Twentieth-Century Lace

1   Luba Krecji at work on a needlepoint lace, using
a special technique that she has developed herself.
Specimens of her work are illustrated on pp. 150–2.

Ernst-Erik Pfannschmidt
Architekt D.A.I. Baurat Dipl. Ing.

Twentieth-Century Lace

MILLS & BOON LIMITED, LONDON

First published in Great Britain 1975 by
Mills & Boon Limited, 17–19 Foley Street,
London W1A 1DR

ISBN 0 263 05627 9

By the same author:
FOUNTAINS AND SPRINGS (published by
George G. Harrap & Co Ltd)
METAL FURNITURE (published by
Julius Hoffmann Verlag, Stuttgart)

ACKNOWLEDGEMENTS

The author and publishers would like to thank Mrs Sybil Allan, of Sheffield, for kindly reading
the English script and making many helpful suggestions, and for providing the photographs of
English work; also Mr Gardner, Librarian of the Embroiderers Guild, for contributing a book
list.
Thanks are also due to Frl. Koch, of Alexander Koch, Publishers, who put at the author's
disposal the unpublished work of Emma von Sichart.
The cover picture, "Rainbow Couch", 1973, is by Sherri Smith, U.S.A.

Made and printed in Great Britain by
Butler & Tanner Ltd, Frome and London

Contents

Dedication

I dedicate this book to my mother, who introduced me to lace-making when I was quite young. I now know that what she most wanted to teach me was not manual skill but the habit of perseverance. The art of lace-making also sharpened my sense of touch, which, like some of our other senses, tends to be blunted by the effect of our modern environment. Finally, my mother opened my eyes to the beauty of lace. For that alone, I shall always be grateful.

Secondly, I dedicate this book to every artist in lace in any part of the world who designs beautiful patterns and generally executes them himself or herself, often in conditions of real hardship. All too often, these artists know nothing of one another. In this book, for the first time, some of them appear side by side. They represent the creative powers on which our machine age is built. I should also like to thank those artists who made information and photographs available to me. All the work published in this book is protected by the existing art copyright laws. None of it may be reproduced for gain in either handmade or machine-made form.

Finally, I dedicate this book to all who believe in the immortal quality of lace.

I have not attempted to write a textbook of the various techniques used in making lace. Handbooks for experts are available in plenty. (Some suggestions for further reading are given in Appendix I.) Nor have I attempted to write a complete history—much too vast a task. The historical notes that follow are only to put into perspective the main theme of the book, and to point the way to recent developments that have, as far as I know, not been systematically recorded hitherto.

The term "lace" has been interpreted as widely as possible, in order to demonstrate the direction of this form of art. The traditional lace will always deserve our admiration, but modern lace has made its appearance. Where it will go from here, we cannot tell. We can only observe.

Lace-making New and Old

In 1971, I visited a travelling exhibition of Polish "avant-garde" artists. They were showing textile structures executed on a very large scale. Some of them were several metres high, with openings large enough to walk through—not exactly the kind of thing one associates with delicate trimmings. And yet, as I looked more closely at these interesting objects, I discovered that they incorporated ancient braiding techniques—for instance, macramé, plaited cords, fishermen's netting etc. Even these progressive spirits were compelled to draw on the methods and crafts of their forebears.

The oldest forms of netting found in Europe are believed to be the hair nets found on the bodies recovered from the Satrupholm bog near Schleswig. This Ertebølle culture is dated 3,000–4,000 years B.C.

A perfectly circular piece of netting, relatively well preserved, was found in Egypt, in a Roman grave. It is an amazing piece of work—it looks like 20th-century lace.

There is a well-preserved mural in the Doge's Palace in Venice. It was painted by Paolo Veronese and shows the virtues of patience and industry, holding a large cobweb—a memorial to the many lace-makers who made their contribution to the wealth of the City-State of Venice.

It is no coincidence that the principal contenders for the honour of being the cradles of lace-making are invariably ports, such as Venice or Bruges. In Çatal Hüyük, Turkey, the net was used to catch birds and small mammals. By the sea, the fishing industry stimulated a continual improvement in net-making.

Veronese's fine mural is more than an allegory. The Überseemuseum in Bremen displays a scooping net actually made from cobwebs. It was used to catch very small fish.

From its beginnings in the early days of human culture, lace-making developed into a sophisticated craft. Lace became a status symbol and remained so for a long time. The canopy for a fourposter of the Duchesse de la Ferté cost 40,000 francs, and the trousseau for a French princess, in 1739, no less than 625,000 francs. A King of England, William III, is said to have spent £2,459 on lace in a single year (1695) and Madame de Pompadour is said to have paid 60,000 marks for a lace dress. The lace for the wedding clothes of Queen Victoria, in 1840, cost around £1,000.

It is not easy to express the purchasing power of these sums in the currency of today. But even an approximate conversion allows one to appreciate the economic importance of lace, produced both by industrious convents and secular factories. The lace museums of Brussels and St Gallen have some superb examples of the craft.

In the 19th century, it became possible to make lace by machine, or by the action of caustic chemicals. This meant that the lace-makers no longer had to work in unheated, humid cowsheds or similar places so that the delicate thread would not break in the course of the work. Machine work was not only healthier, it also became better paid in the course of the years. A social conscience tends to cloud one's enjoyment of classical lace. It is not always possible to banish the thought of the suffering, exploited and often sick people who made it.

The Re-birth of Hand-made Lace : Italy

Strangely enough, a new impulse in lace-making sprang from a natural disaster. In 1878, heavy rains in Northern Italy caused flooding of the lagoons near Venice. For many weeks, the fishermen could not set out to sea. The result was famine in the islands cut off from the mainland.

To make certain that the islands should never again depend on only one source of income, Queen Margherita, consort of Victor Emanuel I of Italy, founded a school of lace-making on the largest of the islands, Burano.

In the 17th century, Burano had been the seat of a flourishing lace industry. Now, there was only one old lace-maker left alive. Her name was Centa Scapariola, and she was 70 years old. In her youth, she had made needle laces but now she was too old to teach.

The queen unravelled her own old laces in order to discover forgotten stitches and knots. At her request, society ladies with an interest in needlework sat by Centa Scapariola and watched her at her work to try to learn her skill. Needlework teachers were trained who in turn, under the supervision of the Countess Marcello, taught the art of needlemade laces to many girls, from the age of 13 upwards.

In addition, a special course was devoted to the design of new laces. Frequently iris-type flowers and vigorous flowing ornaments, in the manner popular at the turn of the century, were worked on handmade net in the style of Alençon lace. In addition to these national schools of lace-making, there were private ventures, for instance, Jesurum in Venice, and Olga Asta. In her unpublished work, Emma von Sichart mentions Falcone in Sicily, Macomer of Cagliari, Sardinia, Casalguidi of Pistoia and the lace-making school at Castle Racconigi, as makers of particularly good copies of antique laces.

After World War I, it was found that the old, valuable laces were out of tune with the contemporary style of living. This enabled Italy to make her contribution to the development of modern, essentially 20th-century lace.

Bobbin lace in the new style was made at Cantu, under the management of Wenter Marini. Crombelli concentrated on needlemade lace, Giulio Rosso of Verona on net embroidery.

At long last, the Italian government began to support the work by the foundation of a special institute for the promotion of handicrafts (ENAPI). This was a mixed technique, with flower motifs in needlepoint being mounted on a foundation of crochet net. The designers were Gino Foltrani and Virgilio Guzzi Melotti.

Now, Venice is not the only great port with a tradition of net-making, i.e. the basis of lace-making. We must not forget Genoa, and the very fine bobbin lace from Santa Margherita.

As an important item in ladies' fashion, Italian lace was greatly encouraged by the national fashion authority in Turin. The year 1949 saw the emergence of new names that are worth remembering; for instance, Pia di Valmarana-Saonnaria-Padua, and Fabbrici Clerici.

Jesurum alone, in their factories in Chioggia, Palestrina, Burano and the other small islands near Venice, gave employment to up to 500 lace-workers. These women made not only needlepoint laces but also "shadow embroidery" which was used, among other things, for delicate tea-table sets of the finest coloured organdy. In 1941, after many years of preparation, another important school of lace-making was opened by the Princess of Piedmont in Racconigi. Here, too, efforts were made to shorten the time-consuming part of lace-making by using a mixed technique of needlepoint and bobbin lace.

Annual exhibitions are held on a considerable scale where bobbin lace from Sansepolcro may be seen together with shadow embroidery from Rovereto, net embroideries from Perugia, "Ars Panicalensis", filet laces from Turin, and other work.

It is interesting to note that the changes in Italy are not confined to the taste in art but extend to the social conditions of the lace workers. In the School of Lace-Making of Burano, for instance, regulations ensure that the workrooms are kept scrupulously clean and are whitewashed annually. Careful attention is paid to the health of the women. If one of them falls ill, her work is burnt, regardless of its value. Every woman has her workbook in which her output is recorded, together with the selling price of each finished piece. The school takes only a small commission.

It may be of interest to end this section with some indication of the time needed for lace-making, which may make it easier to understand why such high prices are charged for christening robes, bridal gowns etc.

In 1942, a triangular mantilla was made for the Milan Triennale. It was worked in black silk and measured 1·20 metres by 2·60 metres ($47\frac{1}{2}$ by $102\frac{1}{2}$ in.). It took three women one year and six months. The mantilla was worked in three parts which were subsequently joined with invisible lace stitches. It weighed 100 grammes (little more than 3 oz.). It was designed by Professor Franco Bossi, who designed for the bobbin lace school of Cantu.

Development in Belgium

Development in Belgium was along similar lines. In order to aid the Flemish lace industry, Queen Elizabeth of Belgium gave her patronage to a Lace Ball which was attended by the entire Court, as well as by representatives of the nobility, the diplomatic corps and the world of commerce. This was in 1918. The queen wore a dress of gold-embroidered Brussels lace and a cloak of Flemish lace. A resplendent parade illustrated the history of lace.

The convents opened new lace-making schools, for in Belgium, too, skilled lace workers had become almost extinct. In 1911, schools were founded in Turnhout and Alost. It is reported that in 1914, the lace-making industry in Bruges, Mechelen, Courtrai, Grammont, and Ypres employed 41,000 women. By 1949, there were only 10,000 women operating the lace-making machines and looms in seven factories in Brussels, Ninove and Vilvorde. There is no record, however, of the women who worked in their own homes. Most of their work was done in the winter, when there was not so much to do outside on the farm (Emma von Sichart). Turnhout is known for its "Malines" or "Mechlin" and "Point de Paris", Lille and Bruges for "Binche" and "Valenciennes", and Termonde and the surrounding area is associated with "Duchesse" and "Appliqué".

The very names of these laces show that they are traditional styles that are not really the subject of this book. Even the opening of a new school for bobbin lace in Bruges failed to stimulate new creative powers in Belgium. Exports account for 95% of the Belgian lace production. Unfortunately it is a case of quantity at the expense of quality. This mass-produced work is a long way from the beauty of the bedspread presented to the Archduke Albert of Flanders and his bride, Isabella, on their marriage in 1599 (see pp. 51–3). This tradition was continued not in Belgium, but in Bohemia.

Lace in England

English needlework had reached a high standard as early as the 11th century, and the famous Bayeux "Tapestry" is thought to be English work. The early history of lace-making is more obscure. Silk veils, netted and embroidered, with silk motifs, have been dated as early as 1092. Metal laces were in existence when Katharine of Aragon married Arthur, Prince of Wales, in 1501, and there is a tradition that England is indebted to her for the laces of Bedfordshire.

In the 17th century, Flemish refugees settled in England especially in the south-west, including Honiton, Devon. Mrs Neville-Jackson believes that the lace known as "point d'Angleterre" was in fact made by them in England. It is a feature of this type of lace that the pattern is worked first, with bobbins, and the ground is then worked round the design. The threads are looped through the braid of the toile (Emma von Sichart).

At one time, one could actually tell a man's religion by the lace he wore. The Puritans wore a needlepoint lace christened "Holy Point" or "Hollie", the pattern of which was worked in small loops which created a close mesh ground. The Catholics, on the other hand, were allowed to indulge in more luxurious "vanities". Openwork shirts cost £5, £10 or even £100. When such extravagance was made an offence, the lace-workers appealed to the Pope himself to get the ban revoked.

Lace was an important feature of both male and female dress in the 17th and 18th centuries, and remained popular with women after men's costume had become more austere. Mrs Elton in Jane Austen's *Emma* (1815) contemptuously dismisses a wedding that could display only "very few lace veils", and lace flounces and shawls were prized by Victorian ladies.

Ireland did not produce a lace of her own until the 19th century. Irish crochet is based on the patterns and effects of needlepoint. Raised flowers and sprigs were mounted separately on a picot-decorated ground, to give the effect of Venetian rosepoint. Some of these padded sprays were produced in Burano, Italy, where by 1910 they had become a sufficiently big export item to keep a whole industry going.

The craft, carried on by working women, was literally worth its weight in gold. Anyone wanting to buy fine handmade net had to cover the piece with shillings. Needless to say, the position changed with the appearance of machine-made netting.

Limerick lace was first made about 1820. This and another Irish lace, Carrickmacross, are very closely allied to embroidery, and the distinctions between the various kinds, though fascinating, are outside the scope of this book.

1891 saw the foundation of the "East Devon Lace Industry", the "Home Art Industry", the "Midland Lace Association" and the "Buckingham Lace Association". All this resulted in an improved technique, but it proved more difficult to stimulate the imagination of the designers.

Few, if any, of the regional lace organisations survived the second decade of the 20th century. Change of fashion, lack of workers threatened the skill with extinction. In the lace-making districts it was taught in some schools; elsewhere in convents and, to a very limited extent, in girls' boarding schools. Fortunately, a few old lace-makers continued to work and individuals all over the country helped to keep some interest alive.

Since 1960, an increasing interest has been shown in lace-making as a hobby. Technical and Adult Colleges from Yorkshire to Devon and the Lake District to Oxfordshire now include it in their syllabuses. The Women's Institutes and, to a lesser extent, the Townswomens' Guilds encouraged the art and it would be reasonable to assume that there are now lace-makers in every county. Wales has its own "Society of Wales" with approximately 80 members; Sheffield Lacemakers number 62. The Women's Institutes have an increasing number of applicants for their Lace-making tests and since 1970 have trained a gratifying number of teachers.

Most of today's workers want to work traditionally and a surprising number prefer to work with the finest thread available, although this means very slow progress. There is not yet much interest in large-scale work, but magazines are producing patterns for stoles and scarves, which can be worked with Lurex or other modern threads.

Quarterly auctions of lace now held in London are widening the interest in old lace and introducing the present generation to the charm of its texture and designs. Demonstrations can often be seen at shows and exhibitions.

Some of those who have taken to lace-making quite late in life have reached a very high standard of finished work, enthusiasm making up for the lack of practice. Original designs on the whole keep well within the traditional framework, even that of a farmer's wife who copied her husband's prize "Saddleback" pig (in miniature)!

Lace in Germany

Some time ago, I dialled a Reutlingen number. The telephone rang for a long time but there was no reply. And then, at long last, Leni Matthaei answered herself—and her voice sounded like that of a girl of eighteen. "I'm so sorry to have kept you waiting—I was working at my lace and I simply couldn't break off just then—oh yes, I'm at my work every day, for all that I'm 93 years old . . ."

Some years earlier, I had visited this remarkable woman in her Reutlingen home. As a young girl, she had gone to Paris to join a lace-making school, where she had covered a three-year course in as many months. She had completed her training in the Erz mountains. Gifted with a rare feeling for art, she has always been part of the contemporary scene. Her laces have brought her many awards, including, in 1972, the National Prize awarded at Constance, West Germany. When her life's work was burnt in the war she, nothing daunted, began all over again.

"Of all types of lace," Leni Matthaei once wrote, "I think bobbin lace is technically the most interesting. A needle is so rigid, and knots remind me of haberdashery. But bobbins are mobile . . . bobbin work gives you greater scope with regard to movement and the sensitivity of the woven threads in combining into a pattern." It was one of Leni Matthaei's achievements to do away with the distinction between net ground and "motif". She has an uncanny way of presenting, in an abstract form, drops of water, snow crystals, or the growing of a plant, and all these objects take on a mysterious life of their own.

On 23 February, 1968, Frau Matthaei wrote me a long letter, of which I should like to quote the following paragraph:

"The only 'genuine laces' I recognise are

> needlepoint laces
> and bobbin laces.

In my opinion, their net ground is not related to the fisherman's net—I don't see how they can possibly be, since they are based on a continuous thread, and—in the great majority of cases—are worked together with the pattern, as opposed to 'filet lace'. Nor can the French net ground have evolved from the fisherman's net; it is made with bobbins or a needle, and in a continuous pattern. It is possible that there is a connection between filet lace and fisherman's netting."

In 1907, Frau Matthaei had to go to Paris to learn her craft. The German lace-making schools made their appearance somewhat later with government aid. Special mention must be made of the colleges at Stadlern, Tiefenbach, Schönsee and Nordhalben, in the borderland of Bavaria. Another college was opened in Hirschberg, in Silesia. The small, Schleswig town of Tondern had several lace-making schools, and even in Berlin, a "German School of Lace-making" came into being.

Frau Laura Eberhard taught lace-making at the Kunstgewerbeschule (College for Arts and Crafts) Stuttgart, Professor Czeschka was in charge in Hamburg, and Professor Else Jaskolla in Munich. She made the Signs of the Zodiac Cloth that is now in the Neue Sammlung in Munich (page 120).

In third place, after Frau Matthaei and Frau Jaskolla, we must pay tribute to Frau Johanna Harre, of Hanover. A past mistress of the cloth stitch, Frau Harre does not use the half-stitch in her bobbin laces but achieves smooth surfaces and delicate shadings by means of the cloth stitch. She too was a teacher at one time, at the lace-making school in Hildesheim.

I tried, unsuccessfully, to see Grete Thums in Vienna, and soon afterwards she died. She had originally been a hand weaver and studied under Professor Wimmer in Vienna. Some very fine laces made by her are now in the Austrian Museum for Applied Art. As she wrote to me after my attempt to see her, she works without a pattern, "from the depth of her mind". In a letter she addressed to me on 20 September 1967, she wrote as follows:

"I should like to reply to your question about my technique if only I knew the answer . . .

How does the ultra-fine linen thread turn into a delicate fabric full of life, movement and expression, merely by means of crossing and twisting? I am filled with the wish to bring it to life as it lives in me. When a design has taken possession of me, I carry it around till it is clear in every detail. Then I commit it to blue squared paper (because the threads show up better) but only the outline. First comes the frame, in which the weave is suspended. I begin at the lower edge and build upwards. The bobbins are pinned to the pillow, and then the wonderful work can commence, a rewarding game, rather like an orchestra, where every bobbin has its part, and they combine and solve all problems. My hands transmit the will and the power to control each bobbin. And as if by a miracle, the longed-for result is before me, according to my will, my imagination, and I am amazed.

But is very difficult work that makes great demands on patience, nerves, endurance and calmness (Ruhe). There is often confusion, restlessness, trial and error, groping till things come right, and then the sigh of relief to have got one's desire.

I should like to illustrate one such point. In the picture called 'The Garden of Eden' look at the glance of the serpent at Eve—what expression! I shall never know—wherefrom, how, why???" (Illustration p. 130)

There is nothing one can add to the words of this modest artist. The difference between hand lace and machine lace will never be put better.

After World War II, the Bavarian lace schools had the good fortune to find an artistic adviser in Suse Bernuth, who produced a large number of designs. By the use of Lurex gold and coloured linen threads, she has revived ancient techniques. As in the case of Grete Thums, her figured laces are of particular interest. They are among the best laces that have been made in this century.

14

Lace in Eastern Europe

As we have seen earlier, lace developed early in Italy. Dalmatia provided the bridge to eastern Europe. The Ragusa lace of the 16th and 17th centuries vied bitterly with that produced in the Venetian Republic. The convents in Dalmatia worked primarily for the churches and for the national dress, right to the beginning of the 20th century. This prevented the tradition from dying out, as was the case elsewhere. The patterns were copied as far as Asia. The ornamentation draws on its Phoenician/Mycenean origin. Even the name of the technique—"ivory technique"—"punto avorio", also called "punto dei greci" and sometimes "punto sarazeno", is indicative of the age. These were three-dimensional laces, with a knotted stitch. The manufacture of these valuable "Ragusa" laces did not extend beyond the 18th century.

New schools for lace-making were obviously called for in this part of the world—Spalato, Pago and Capocesia. Frau Natalie von Bruck-Auffenberg has commemorated these laces in her book *Dalmatinische Volkskunst*, published by Schroll, Vienna.

In 1890, the Imperial Central School of Lace-making was founded in Vienna, under the artistic supervision of Dr Josef Stark, together with the Central Teaching Institute for home industries for women. In the course of time, the latter became responsible for approximately 40 schools of lace-making. Such well-known names in lace-making as, for example, Frau Pleyer of Schönfeld, Frau Richter and Frau Janninger in Gottesgab quickly raised the standard of Austrian lace to the highest level of craftsmanship. In Austria, as the queens had done in Italy and Belgium, the Empress herself took an active interest in the craft of lace-making and took a hand when state subsidies were needed. At the Paris Exhibition in 1900, laces made in accordance with the designs of Hradlicka and Franziska Hofmann-ninger, were awarded the "Pour le Mérite".

Hungary was subjected to repeated Turkish invasions in the 15th and early 16th centuries. During this time, very valuable laces were made of gold and silver threads, but, unfortunately, not much has survived. As a result of the wars, lace-makers had left the towns for the country, and they worked away in quiet villages, unaffected by fashionable trends.

At the beginning of this century, an art teacher from Kiskunhalas had the audacity to develop a contemporary Hungarian lace. His name was Arpad Dekani (1861–1931), and he found a very gifted colleague in Maria Markovits. Their "Halas lace", a needlepoint, appeared for the first time, in Hungary, in 1902. The pattern was made by darning stitches that resembled fine linen. These laces are the purest Art Nouveau, consciously 20th century, and, with the rediscovery of Art Nouveau, they too are inevitable coming back into favour. Maria Csernyanszky describes the further development in her book *Ungarische Spitzenkunst*, published by Corvina Verlag. The more serious student will find it well worth his while to read this book. In the meantime, we must refer to the extraordinary achievements of Maria Markovits and Dekani and to the "Hunnia" lace of Frau A. Fay. After the collapse of the Danube monarchy, the lace schools in the new Republic of Czechoslovakia were controlled by the Staats-Schulanstalt für Hausindustrie (National Educational Institute for Home Industry) in Prague.

The Director, Karl Vlaczek, was successful in obtaining the services of Emilie Paličkova, whose work as a designer has reached a standard as yet unequalled in the history of modern lace. In 1962, she was the subject of a monograph by Ludmilla Kybalovà. We reproduce a few illustrations from this beautifully illustrated book, pp. 91, 122–5, 148. Emma von Sichart wrote, in her unfortunately unpublished book on lace: "When I look at the work of Frau Emilie Paličkova, a whole world of marvels comes into view: fabulous animals, fairyland flowers, set in a background of imaginative, fluid forms that seem to rise and fall in a rhythmic movement; joined together by all means open to art. Perhaps the most beautiful work of them all is a cloth with a diameter of 1·20 metres ($47\frac{1}{2}$ in.). Concentric circles and radial lines form a rounded cobweb from which arise delicate grass blades and flower stalks: The effect suggests a summer wind rippling through corn, or flowers in a summer meadow nodding against the sky. There is something awe-inspiring in a skill that can conjure up such visions with linen thread and bobbins."

In 1939, Professor Ferdinand Staeger exhibited the Mozart Cloth in the Haus der Deutschen Kunst (House of German Art), in Munich. Sixteen women employed by the School of Lace in Schönfeld needed a total of 15,800 working hours to make it. The teacher who supervised the work was Miss Horner. Professor Ludwig Renner designed the "Venus Cloth" and the "Four Seasons".

Luba Krejci uses two different techniques, bobbin lace and needle lace, for her wall hangings. The needlepoint lace is worked without a pattern—without a preconceived design or even a sketch. The ground net is a kind of weave with asymmetric warp and weft. The pattern is produced by a variety of knotting techniques. The bobbin lace wall hangings are designed as pictures, freely suspended from the top edge.

This artist had been working in this manner ever since 1947, but it was not until 1959 that her lace hanging "Carnival" made her name overnight. Her third lace hanging "We carry the Sun to the Stars" received the gold medal in the 1960 Triennale in Milan. She executes the entire work by herself in linen and hemp thread. (Illustrations, frontispiece, pp. 16, 150–2.)

Her work has been shown in Antwerp, Buenos Aires, Florence, Leningrad, London, Manchester, Moscow, Munich, New York, Ottawa, Reval, Riga, Santiago de Chile, Stockholm, Stuttgart, Warsaw and Winnipeg. This wide diffusion confirms the growing interest in contemporary lace, nowhere more so than among architects for whom this is a new medium offering new possibilities.

16

Fashion as Patron

By 1913, world fashion had once more become the patron of lace. Whole dresses were made of Venetian lace, of ribbons or Irish crochet. There were lace jackets, gloves, muffs, parasols and hats trimmed with lace, quite apart from enormous use of lace for personal and household linen. Accessories such as bows, sofa cushions and lampshades were in great demand.

Major lace exhibitions were being held in Berlin, Munich, Darmstadt, Hanover, Mannheim, Flensburg, Kiel and Trier at frequent intervals. A special lace museum was founded in Plauen.

The first impetus may have come from the exhibition of the Paris Musée des Arts Décoratifs (Decorative Arts Museum) which was held in 1911. A very remarkable collection of French and Italian laces in the latest style were on show. Some of Frau Selmersheim's Art Nouveau laces are popular even now.

In Britain, the tea gown came into fashion, a flowing garment with a barely noticeable waist line below the bosom, inspired by pre-Raphaelite ideals. In Germany, the tea gown turned into the "reform dress". And this called for new laces.

It is hardly surprising that around the turn of the century, Alexander Koch of Darmstadt decided to publish a *Deutsche Stickerei und Spitzenzeitung* (German news of embroidery and lace). This excellent periodical fell a victim to the paper shortage in 1943. After the war, people were fighting for survival. Lace was very low down on the list of priorities.

In talking of Alexander Koch, we must not forget that it was his idea to found a colony of artists at Mathildenhöhe near Darmstadt, with studios and living accommodation for artists. In 1902, the idea became a reality. The first exhibition held at Mathildenhöhe was a worldwide success.

In Vienna, Joseph von Hoffmann founded the "Vienna Workshops" (Wiener Werkstatte) in 1903. They were killed off by the economic crisis in 1932. An exhibition held by the Austrian Museum for Applied Art in 1967 showed what had been achieved at the Workshops. There were workshops for silver, gold and other metals, for tin and enamel, leather goods and bookbinding, for fashion and knitting, beadwork, embroidery, textile painting, and pottery of every kind; fabrics, woven and printed, carpets, wallpapers, and printed silks were produced in first-class factories associated with the Workshops. Laces and smaller knitwear were made by homeworkers.

The Vienna Workshops have cradled many important artists. Dagobert Peche, born 1887 in St Michael, Salzburg, died 1923, was probably the most versatile designer who worked there. His is the beautiful saying: "Art is the endeavour to sense the invisible rhythms that surround us, to discover their law, to turn chaos to order."

I was successful in getting in touch with the former Managing Director of the Vienna Workshops, Max Bude. He gave me the design sketches by Dagobert Peche shown on pp. 64–6, together with a large number of photographs for my archives; for instance, of the collection of ribbon designs of the Vienna Workshops. This enables us to admire the talent for improvisation that Peche displays in his tulle embroideries.

Threads used in Lace-making

The "Ohrenburg shawls" worn by the Cossack women in Russia, could be pulled through a wedding ring. That is the kind of fact that makes one's mind turn to the materials used in lace-making.

In the early days of lace, silk or metal threads were widely used. Trimmings of silk or gold thread present one big problem, however— they are difficult to clean. The white linen thread became popular in the 16th century.

Anyone who has visited Egypt will have watched the women who by incessant movement of the right hand, keep a thread in motion and turn it into a fine twist that automatically rolls itself on to a freely suspended spindle. By the same method, the Egyptian women of 4,000 years ago were able to produce a thread of incredible fineness. It is a fact that no machine will ever produce a thread to match that made by this hand-driven "whorl".

Much linen thread comes from Great Britain. Northern Ireland in particular has (like the Low Countries) the moist climate that produces the best flax and consequently the best linen. Lawn bleaching gives Irish linen its soft shade that is so much more attractive than the glaring white of the German thread.

Valenciennes used to be charged at 500 to 2,000 francs per pound. It was first measured and then weighed. The terms used for costing are based on an English system. The terms are English, and the prices in £-Sterling. These fine lace threads have their own number system which is quite different from that used for ordinary sewing cotton.

Around 1838, the costly linen thread began to be replaced progressively by cheaper cotton threads, much to the detriment of the lace.

Cotton is stiffer, less supple in use, but it has contributed to the success of machine lace. Rayon thread too has something rigid about it. In France and Italy very finely spun wool has been used in bobbin lace and mantillas.

The Emergence of Bobbin Lace

Although the origin of lace will probably never be known with certainty, there is a school of thought that believes it to derive from fishermen's nets—and to me this is entirely convincing.

Modern artists in lace are basing their textile structures to an ever-growing degree on the earliest methods. For this reason, we have to devote a little time to the technical aspect of lace. This book is not written only for makers or collectors of lace, nor for designers, commercial artists, stage designers or architects, although they may find in it some ideas that they can translate into their own media. But over and above that, I am hoping that this book will guide many people to a world of beauty which they did not know existed. Hardly anyone can fail to derive some superficial, aesthetic satisfaction from looking at lace, but real appreciation is not possible without some knowledge of the techniques involved.

It is possible to produce a net without any knots, merely by interlooping and twisting. A prehistoric piece of netting made by double looping can be seen in the National Museum in Copenhagen.

In the Musée de l'Homme (Anthropological Museum) in Paris, you can see the edge of a hoop-net made with deep-piercing loops. I understand they also have an example of the hour-glass technique practised in Guinea.

With these techniques, however, it only needs one broken thread for the whole net to unravel. The knotted net was an inevitable advance. The movability of a knot is dependent on the material. Originally, the knots were immovable. Modern materials are so smooth, however, that the knots became movable and had to be replaced by new types that stayed more firmly in position.

The book *Fischnetzknoten* (fishermen's knots) by Andres von Brandt provides an excellent survey. The simplest form is the lake-dwellers' knot, which can also be seen in the Congo Museum in Tervuren, near Brussels.

The cross knot was known to the Incas of Peru. It is a mesh always used when tension has to be compensated in a piece of netting. This technique, with many variations, is the one most commonly used in Africa and Asia.

The weaver's knot is an advance on this. It is also known as Schotenstek or fisherman's knot. Oddly enough, it is used in the hairnet from the Satrupholm bog, mentioned earlier (p. 7) as a very old European find.

The double knot, with ever-changing variations, belongs to modern times. It is rather complicated and accordingly more suitable for hand-made than for machine-made netting.

In view of the fact that some of these knots have been in existence for 8,000 years, it seems almost incredible that even now, patents are being taken out in this field. But the German patents DRP 848 349 and DRP 884 397 are examples.

The above-mentioned bodies from Satrupholm wore not only artistically knotted hairnets, but also borders with a tassel finish, used to fasten their wide garments. The Assyrians used them for the same purpose.

It would seem, therefore, that knotted work first had a functional and later an ornamental purpose. The hems of garments were decorated by pulling out the horizontal threads until the warp had reached a certain length. This was then left as a fringe.

19

This technique came from Arabia to Sicily and Spain and from there to the rest of Europe. By the end of the 13th century, it had become known in Spain as "macramé". The knots, which gave rise to the fringe, are of different kinds. There are raised knots and flat knots, cross knots and weavers' knots, as well as a Chinese knot. Bobbin lace developed from these borders.

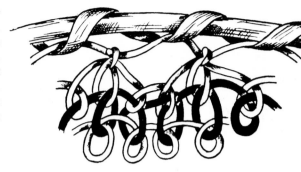

2 Diagrams from the book Fischnetzknoten *(the knotting of fishing nets) by A. von Brandt.*

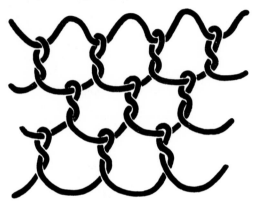

i. Diagram of netting with a double twist. Derived from a piece of Danish prehistoric netting. (National Museum, Copenhagen.)

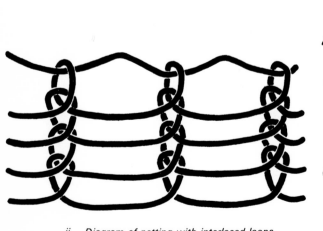

ii. Diagram of netting with interlaced loops.

iii. Diagram showing border of fishing-net and arrangement of loops (Anthropological Museum, Paris).

3 Double knots:

(a) symmetrical with double transverse bends.

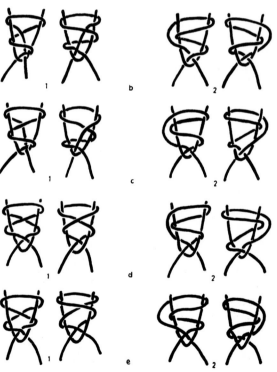

(b–e) Asymmetrical with various means of release (1 from time to time corresponds to 2). Another possibility is shown in diagram IV.

4 Double knots repeatedly interlaced by the shank.

vii. Some divergent forms of knot.

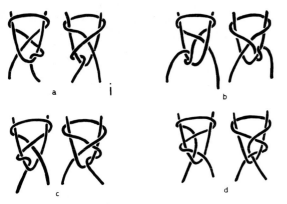

(a–d) the shank encircles the opposite curve of the loop

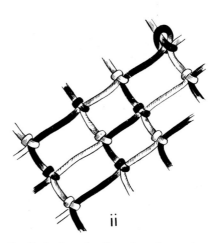

5i. Border of a fishing-net made by lake-dwellers.

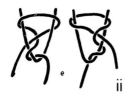

(e) the shank encircles curves of the loop on the same side, and

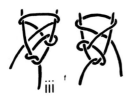

(f) both curves are encircled.

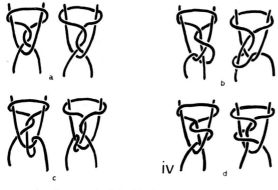

ii. Part of a net with rectangular meshes, made by lake-dwellers.

vi. Symmetrical double knots
    (a) protected by patent—DRP 848 349
    (b–d) derived from the above.

21

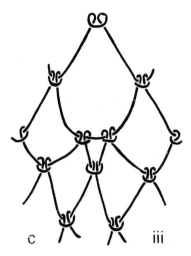

a

6a.   *Lattice net, or half stitch*

iii.   Part of a net with a sliding type of reef knot (the three above from the Congo Museum, Tervuren, Belgium).

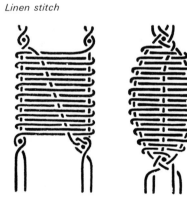

b

iv.   Reef knots
   (a) sliding type
   (b) true reef knots.

b.   *Linen stitch*

c

c.   *Woven plaits*

22

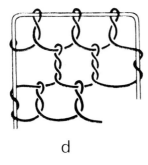

d. Needlepoint double tulle

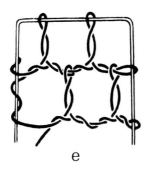

e. Alençon ground needlepoint

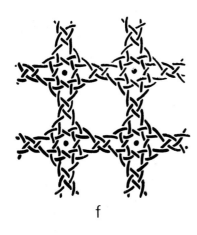

f. Rose ground

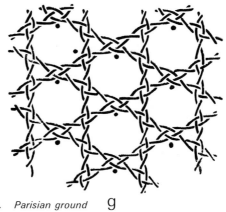

g. Parisian ground

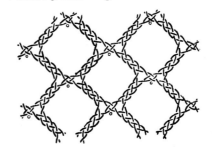

h. Valenciennes ground

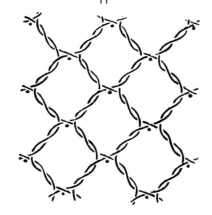

i. "Rijelse" ground

23

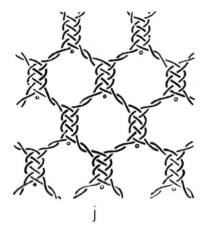

j

j.   Mechlin ground

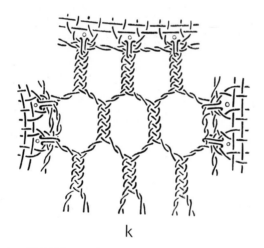

k

k.   Drochel ground

24

The Technique of Bobbin Lace

I am greatly obliged to the Directors of the Provinciaal Museum voor Kunstambachten (the Sterckshof Decorative and Folk Arts Museum) in Deurne–Antwerp, for allowing me to publish a number of excellent enlargements of different stitches used in bobbin lace. It is only by study-ing such photographs that the layman may get an inkling of the potential of this art form.

Professor Kadow also helped me greatly by showing me how he manipulated his bobbins.

Bobbin lace is made basically by twisting, crossing or plaiting pairs of threads. The work

7   Bobbins and pillow for bobbin lace. Bobbin laces are also sometimes made on a revolving pillow. *Photo by W. Alexander, Blisworth, Northampton, England.*

is done on a lace pillow either of elongated roundish form or a weighted roll on a wooden stand. The bobbins are longish pieces of wood on which the thread is wound. The number needed depends on the pattern and may be anything from 6 to 800 pairs. The pattern is produced by the interchange of different kinds of stitches. To hold the threads in place pins are placed at crossing-points in the pre-pricked pattern.

Four bobbins make a stitch. Passing the left over the right is called ''crossing'' and passing the right over the left is called ''twisting'' (or turning). A plait is formed by twisting both outer pairs and then crossing the centre pair indefinitely. From these two simple movements have developed ''half stitch'' and ''whole stitch''. When used to form a solid part of the design they are known respectively as ''net'' and ''cloth''. The openwork grounds and meshes are also made with a varying number of twists and crossings.

Until the end of the 16th century, only these simple stitches and plaiting were used. After that the weaving type of stitch appears in the form known as barleycorn, square, leaf or leaf-work, etc. (Tally, Wheatear, Cornseed, Plait). In the first half of the 17th century, cloth stitch was first used for motifs; these were joined by twisted brides or plaits.

The mesh stitches formed the basis of net foundations. There are many forms—simple mesh, rose net ground, double mesh, torchon, Brussels guipure ground, etc.

These techniques have given the various types of bobbin laces their names. They succeed each other in time. In all about 24 different kinds of bobbin stitches have become known, which must not be mixed up with the different net grounds which were used in turn as a foundation for lace.

In the net ground lace the pattern is worked in cloth stitch whilst the net ground of the lace is worked in one of the above-mentioned meshes.

The early bobbin laces were fairly solid but they became progressively more dainty and transparent. They not only have a net ground

but in addition the motifs contain different forms of ''fillings'' worked in mesh stitches or plaits.

I found some very old bobbin laces in an exhibition held at the Sterckshof Museum near Antwerp, in 1967. To me, they seemed much more original than many more recent bobbin laces because they were worked ''free hand'', i.e. without a pattern. Some of these laces are illustrated in the pages that follow (pp. 35–8, 40–6, 48). It is just possible that copies of the exhibition catalogue may still be found in some libraries or specialist museum collections, and it well repays study.

Later came a period when the lace-makers seemed to be chiefly concerned with simplifying and speeding up their time-consuming work—or as we would say nowadays, to rationalise.

In guipure lace, for instance, the warp is made of gimp thread whilst the weft is of linen or silk. Gimps are strips of parchment or carton twined round with silk or metal threads. Needless to say, a strong relief effect can be achieved without much effort.

These braids are connected by brides, or bars, and do not have a mesh foundation. This very old technique readily lends itself to use in modern textiles. We come across a good many cords and tubes of coloured plastic nowadays. These might be described as representing a contemporary version of guipure lace, made with different materials and for different uses.

After that, the combined laces made their appearance, in order to simplify the work still further, and also to produce new effects. In this type, the net ground is worked separately, and the individual motifs, which can be made with bobbins or the needle, are added subsequently.

The combined laces include the ''blondes''. They were originally made in linen thread, later in silk. The pattern, of loosely worked bobbin lace, is picked out and emphasized with a loosely twisted thread. Their colour was at first a milky white, later they were worked in black.

Incidentally, the only time I have ever seen real coloured laces was in the ''Magazin'' of the Austrian Museum for Applied Art, in Vienna.

These were borders made by Cretan peasant women who had probably coloured their threads with different vegetable dyes.

Lately, the technique of coloured bobbin lace has been revived in Czechoslovakia and elsewhere.

A major simplification, and the first step towards a completely machine-made lace, came in the 18th century, when machine-made net appeared on the scene. Known as Tulle netting, after the French town where the machine had been invented, it could at first be produced only in widths of up to 50 cm (about 20 in.). At the end of the 18th century, a Briton by the name of Hammond improved the net-making machine and allowed greater widths to be produced. Finally, machine-made netting was perfected by Heathcoat in 1809, and the appliqué laces made their appearance.

In her beautiful book *Alte Spitzen* (Old Laces) Marie Schuette tells us that the use of machinery in lace-making is really much older. She illustrates a lace-type edging of a baroque filet cloth, made on a kind of box loom. Modern lace artists, as for instance Frau Klöckner-Triebe, have adapted this 17th-century technique with most rewarding results.

Needle-made Lace

The same cities that were famous for the bobbin laces, also produced needlerun or needlepoint laces. These developed from the need to hem a garment. Needle-made lace is older than bobbin lace and only knows a single stitch, the simple buttonhole stitch. It often needs an expert with a magnifying glass to tell whether an old lace was made with needle or bobbins.

Needlepoint is not confined to a particular width and can tackle any task. Modern lace artists, who favour animals, people and whole landscapes and townscapes as subjects, find the needle the more adaptable tool.

Some lace artists, especially in Czechoslovakia, like to work combination laces with bobbin-made braids and needlework filling stitches.

Tulle Lace

Tulle lace has a particular attraction for the Austrian artists in lace. The most recent arrival of the three kinds of lace, it appeared only after the invention of machine-made netting. There are two types of tulle lace. One uses different types of lace stitches in order to produce the effects of needle-point on a supple ground, whilst in the other type, the needle is drawn through the meshes of the delicate net so that the thread forms a variety of flat patterns. These winding lines can conjure up showers of blossoms on the airy ground. The work requires an exact knowledge of the net ground used. Its small, adjacent holes determine the course of the thread and accordingly the design, which should blend perfectly with the ground. By contrast with needle lace, where the pattern must be raised, nothing may project from tulle lace (Emma von Sichart). Tulle lace was principally made in Vienna, Belgium, and in Saxony (Germany). Among the most successful exponents of the art were Sofie Rade and Margarethe Freytag-Just, both of Dresden. They worked free-hand, without first bothering to draw their design on paper, which no doubt accounts for the inimitable originality of their creations. In this connection, we must also mention Frau Neppert-Bohland-Rohl, the Head of the Bavarian School of Embroidery, Naila in Upper Franconia, Frau Anna Gehring of Hameln, Anne-Marie Brocher of Munich, Klein-Filchner and Frau Emmy Zweybrueck-Prohaska.

There is no fabric quite like tulle netting for adorning youth and beauty for the unique occasion, for instance as a bridal gown or a christening robe. Winterhalter, the 19th-century painter of beautiful women in all the courts of Europe, portrayed the Duchess of Montpensier in her Spanish national costume. The dress was made entirely of black lace, worn with lace fan and lace gloves. The national dress of Bohemia and Hungary, too, is even now abundantly trimmed with lace.

Lace in Context

As an architect by profession, I hope I may be permitted a digression, coloured by my personal interests.

The history of architecture teaches us that every style began with heavy, solid forms; then, as the technical know-how increased, shapes became slender and more elegant. Matter becomes progressively less solid. This is an expression of man's ancient longing to free himself from the earth's gravity. No man will ever succeed, but every generation will tackle the problem in its own way. At the moment, it is space travel.

I shall always remember one wonderful day in Freiburg Minster. Of all Gothic churches, this is the one I love best. Its spire is hollow. Lying on the floor below the spire, which is 45 metres high, I looked up into a magnificent lacework of sandstone—a marvellous sensation that I have never recaptured in any other part of the world.

Every traveller will have his own experience of the apparent dissolution of solid matter. In Morocco, there are the "curtain façades" of the casbahs, ornamental walls made up of sun-dried bricks. In Turkey, there are the large, pierced slabs of alabaster that are used in place of glass to let in the light. Anyone who has seen the Alhambra will feel that these Islamic peoples were concerned with more than the materialism with which we are faced every day.

Christian architecture reached its greatest height with the Gothic style. This form owes least to the heritage of antiquity, which can inspire but also restrict. It is an established fact that popular art always lags a few decades behind fine art. Sometimes the gap may be so long that the connection is no longer immediately obvious. That is true of lace that was born of the Gothic style. The Italian laces in particular reflect the finials and rose-windows of the cathedrals.

Lace has followed all other styles in art. We have seen that the classical lace died in the 19th century when the latter was preoccupied with reviving old styles. The century needed its creative powers in order to master its problems elsewhere. The invention of lace-making machinery was not the reason for the decline of the art of lace-making. Today thousands of machines are churning out lace, yet lace as an art form is rising to new heights. For this we are indebted to the machines. The machines have taught us to think about the purpose of work done by hand.

In his book, *Les Quarante Mille Heures,* Fourastier says that in the future, man may have to work no more than 40,000 hours during his life. So much leisure may present its own problem. It is to be hoped that not all man's free time will be spent watching television. It could be that handicrafts will provide the much needed mental equilibrium.

At the "Exposition de l'Art Brut" in Paris in

1967, I saw abstract pictures that had been tatted in several colours, without any design or structure. They were the works of mental patients, the results of occupational therapy, and they struck me as representing a journey into the future.

From Ornament to Structure

A very interesting exhibition was held in Barcelona in 1970: ''Exposicion Internacional de Experiencias Artistico-textiles.'' It was here that I discovered the names of the artists who figure in the final section of this book. They are: Sofie Dawo, born in 1926, Aurelia Munoz b. 1926 and Inge Vahle b. 1915. In 1971, the ''5ème Biennale Internationale de la Tapisserie'' was held in Lausanne. Illustrations are given of work shown there by Marie Vankova, b. 1929, and one item by Maryke Stultiens-Thunissen, b. 1927. I have ventured to include the year of birth because these craftswomen are the avant-garde.

At one time these exhibitions showed the rugs of Lurçat, intended to hang on the wall. Nowadays we find an abundance of abstract structures which our existing vocabulary cannot adequately describe. The words must follow the deeds. On 20 January 1973, Marie Vankova wrote to me from Prague, in a letter that accompanied some photographs:

''In some of these laces I have endeavoured to achieve the three-dimensional effect by other means than in the case of the lace you have seen. For instance, instead of working the lace over the surface of the cylinder for subsequent shaping into a three-dimensional form, I worked the lace direct round a three-dimensional base, e.g. a sphere—and thereby obtained pieces that could not be flattened. In another instance, the three-dimensional lace was made by pulling individual portions of the lace through each other.''

Three-dimensional laces appeared quite early. In the museums, we find baby shoes, caps, bags, gloves, stockings, bridal headpieces and parasols. Most of these pieces, however, had been made up subsequently from pieces of lace that had been conceived and worked as a two-dimensional fabric.

One piece that has been conceived on a three-dimensional basis is a large bouquet of flowers in the Brussels Museum. It was made in approximately the last quarter of the last century.

In West Germany, Professor Hanne-Nüte Kämmerer (Detmold) has courageously extended her work to the very limits of its possibilities. Her work includes a needle-lace portrait of Konrad Adenauer, an astonishing work which does, perhaps, require some getting used to. Her ''Turm der Signale'' was worked with bobbins. ''Seerosen'', on the other hand, was worked as a raised needlepoint.

In 1971, Aurelia Munoz created her ''Komet'' in the ancient macramé lace. One year later she used the same technique in ''Macra Metamorphosis''. Here we have a lace sculpture without any pictorial content.

The works of such artists as these, and of Maryke Stultiens-Thunissen (Holland) and of Inge Vahle (Germany), of Sherri Smith (USA) and others, reflect a new vitality which makes nonsense of forebodings about ''the decline of the West''. This generation believes in the future, and in the necessity of coming to terms with the machine age.

In 1958, especially for the Brussels Exhibition, Marie Vankova-Kuchynkova created a prototype for a white cotton lace for industrial production by Kraja Kraslice. Before long, people will begin to collect machine laces. But that is a subject for another book.

The Classification of Contemporary Lace

Some readers will no doubt have skipped some of the previous pages and others may have complained that they were not nearly detailed enough. But everyone will no doubt have wondered about the evolution and future of contemporary lace.

We live in a "pluralistic" age, in which a variety of views and opinions are allowed to coexist. The modern history of music differentiates four main trends. Perhaps we can apply these divisions to our own field.

The first group is governed by the law of evolution. It is firmly rooted in tradition. The lace-making schools in many countries fall into this category. Anyone wandering along the streets of Sicily will find some fine examples of this attitude, and examples may be found in countries as diverse as England, Russia, Norway, the Netherlands and the USA.

The second group is rooted in the upheaval produced by the impact of Art Nouveau at the turn of the century. In Italy, France and Germany, in Hungary and Bohemia, individual artists were engaging in the search for something new. The type of lace they made has also been produced with great success in the workshops of Vienna. These are real laces, in the traditional sense of the word.

The third group allows the material to explode in all directions. The aim is structure, not ornament. One piece of lace might incorporate a mixture of techniques—everything goes as a means to an end. Representative examples of this type of work can be seen in exhibitions in Germany, Czechoslovakia, Israel and the USA.

The fourth group has no longer anything in common with the traditional lace. The structures have grown into three-dimensional shapes. We are faced with "space knots" which may be large enough to allow one to pass right through them.

These are not the types of lace to make up a veil for the Virgin Mary, or to trim a bridal gown for a queen. They are no longer an aid to fashion. They have become works of art in their own right, often several yards high. The nerves of modern man are progressively less well equipped to make tiny things. The age of space travel is reflected in the human mind.

This development is clearly expressed in contemporary architecture.

The style of our era is referred to as "brutalism". Its characteristic feature is that detail is either lacking or rendered so coarsely that it can be taken in from a moving car. Mouldings are no longer conceived in inches but in feet. The spirit of the age has no time for the pedestrian. Not for us the old-fashioned pleasure of discovering new attractions in the same building by looking at it at different times of the day, or in different seasons. An example may be found in the works of the Hamburg architect Fritz Höger with his Chilehof and Sprinkenhof.

Perhaps these brutal forms are merely an all too honest expression of a brutal age, in which man counts for nothing, or at best as a unit in a plan.

There is a modern textile structure that is suited to the huge, often entirely bare walls of the architect in concrete. In the new Kreishaus in Herzogenbosch in Holland, there is a textile structure—scraping the ceiling—which

32

has left the wall to stand in the room on its own.

Each type of creative work has its place, and it is not the aim of this book to exalt one above another. The author has simply tried to show that lace-making is a craft as vital, as capable of development, as other forms of textile art, and to present examples as a stimulus to workers in search of new ideas.

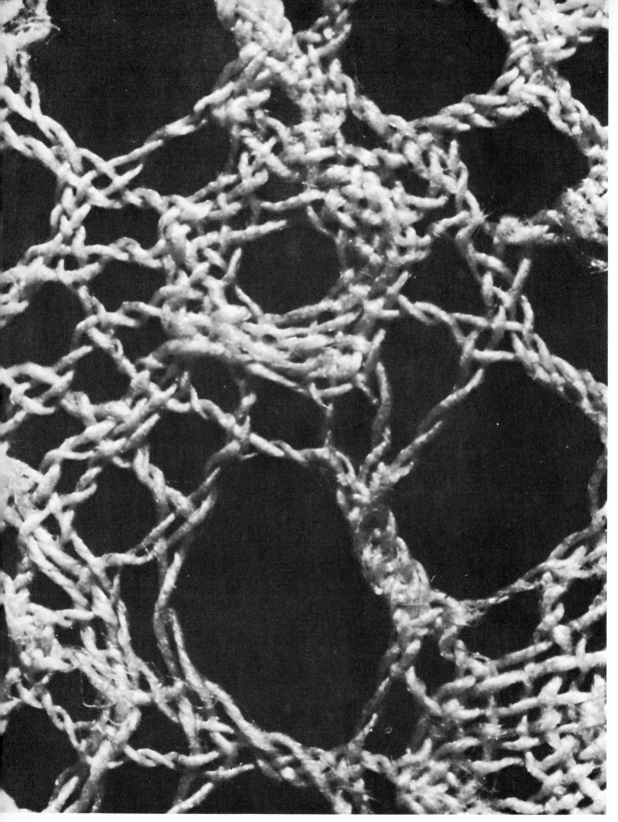

8 Enlarged detail of a so-called ''Old Flemish''
bobbin lace, 17th century. M. Wuyts Collection,
Wijnegem, Belgium. Photo t' Felt, Antwerp.

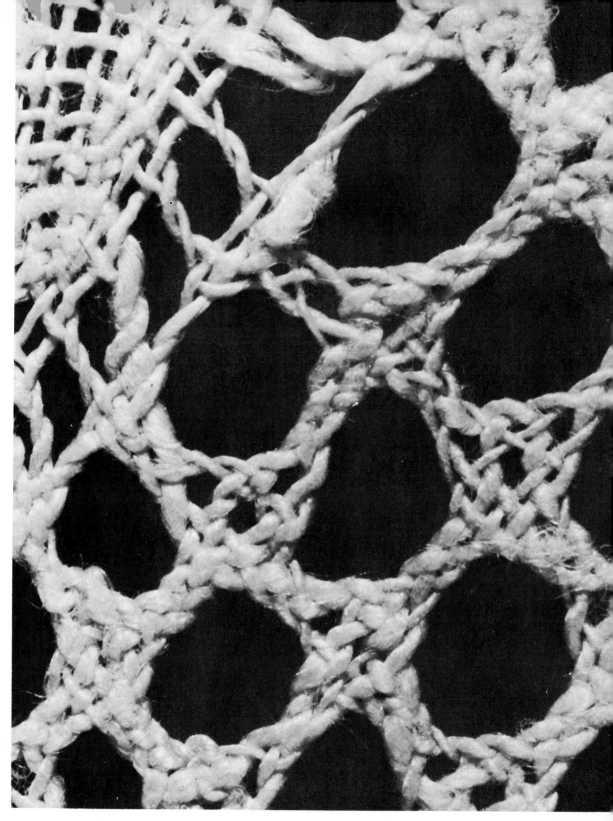

9 Enlarged detail of a bơrder lace from Holland,
first half of 17th century. In the Church of St Carlo
Borromeo. Photo: t' Felt, Antwerp. 35

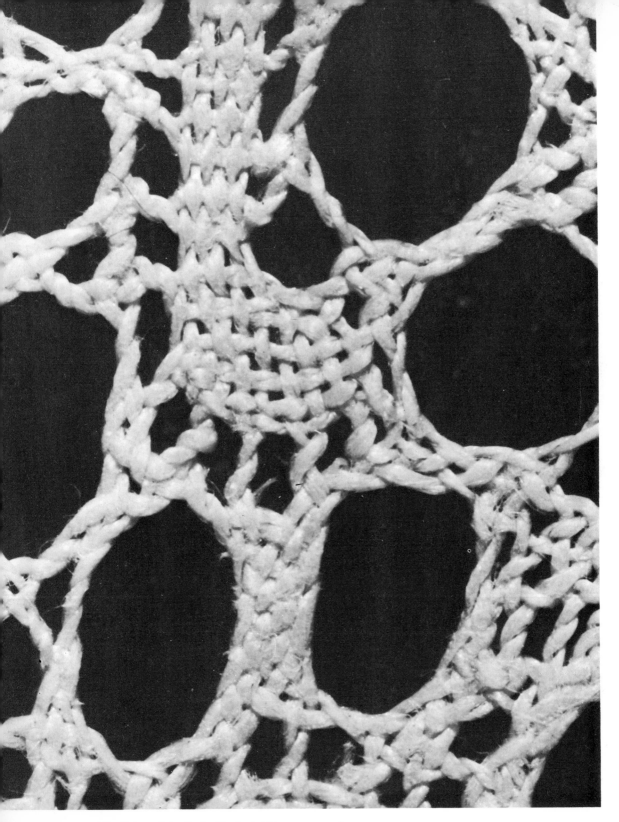

10   Enlarged detail of a Binche bobbin lace, second
half of the 18th century. Originating in the Abbey of
St Bernard, Bornem, Belgium, it is now in the
Sterckshof Museum, Deurne-Antwerp. Photo: t' Felt,
Antwerp.

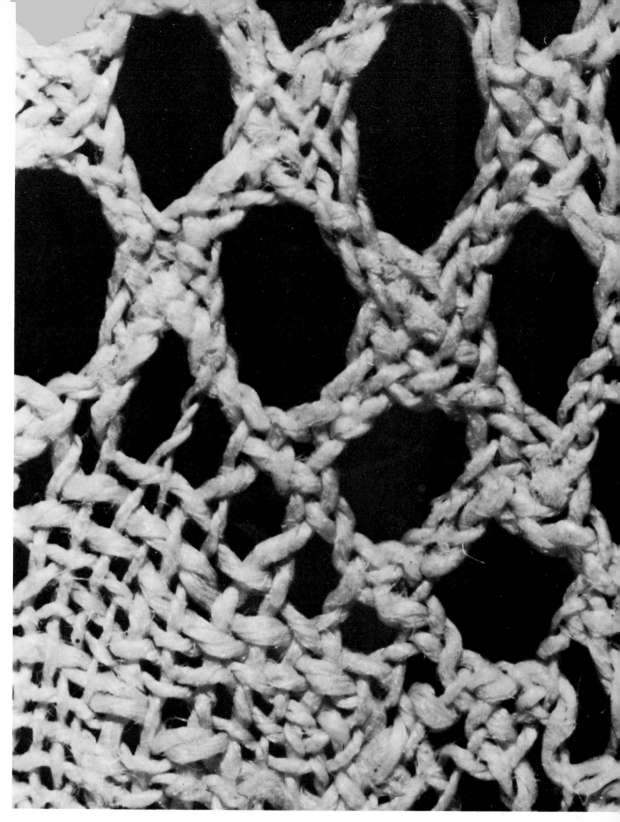

11   Detail of Antwerp bobbin (''plant in pot'') lace
with square mesh. End of 17th century. From the
M. Wuyts Collection, Wijnegem, Belgium. Photo:
t' Felt, Antwerp.

12 Detail of ''Argentan'', French needlepoint lace
with ''lofwerk'' (a special Flemish term that may be
translated as ''leaf work''). 18th century. From M.
Wuyts Collection, Wijnegem. Photo: t' Felt, Antwerp.

38

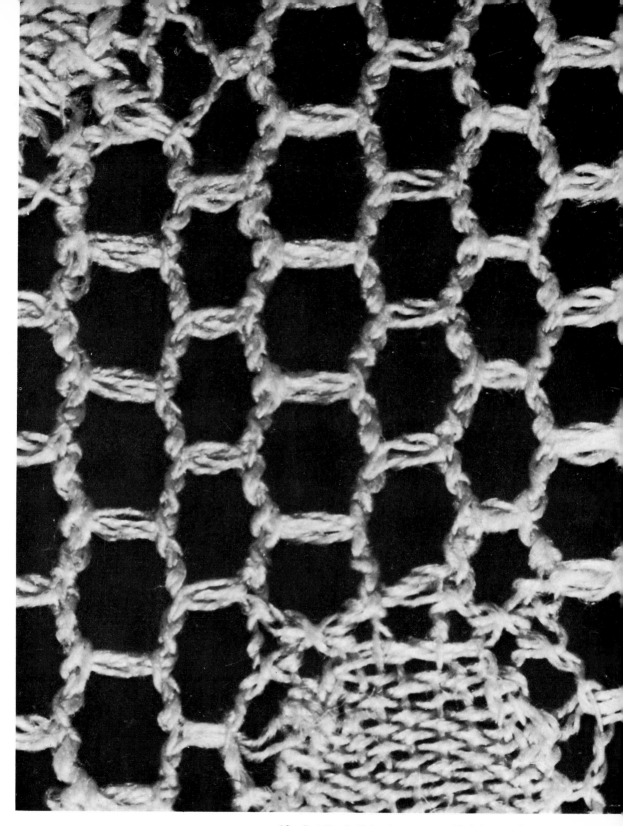

13 Detail of Valenciennes round-holed ground with cloth stitch. 19th century. From the M. Wuyts Collection, Wijnegem, Belgium. Photo: t' Felt, Antwerp.

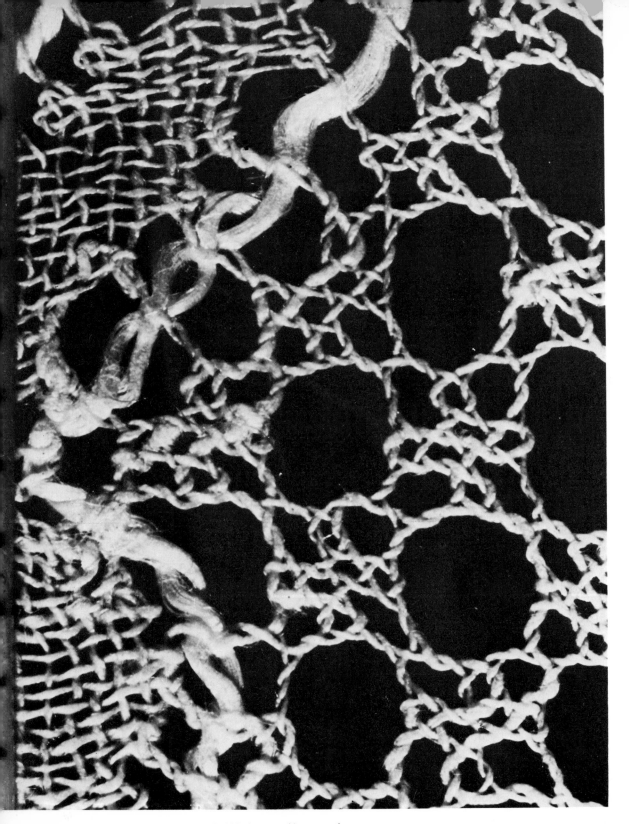

14 Detail of Mechlin bobbin lace, making use of a
fancy ground which resembles a rose-ground. 18th
century. From the M. Wuyts Collection, Wijnegem,
Belgium. Photo: t' Felt, Antwerp.

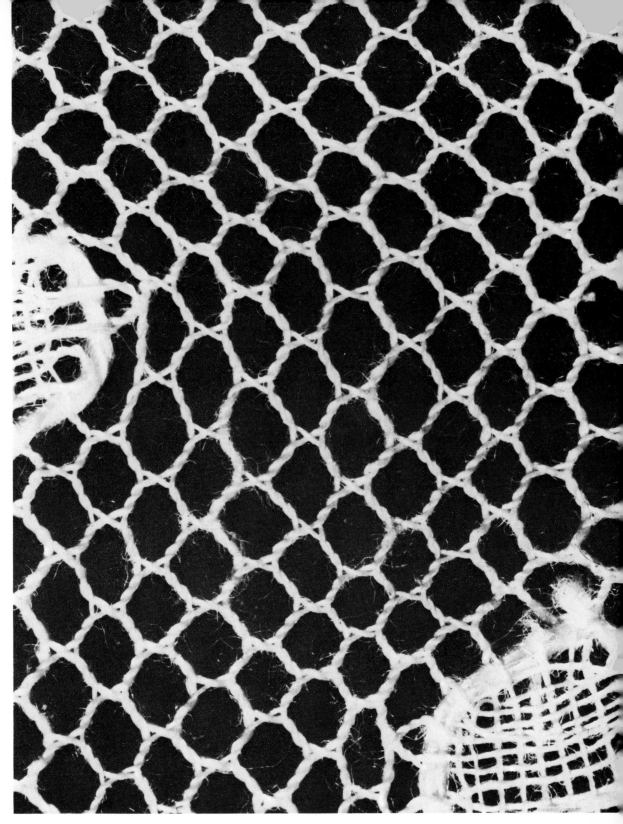

15 *Detail of bobbin lace, Dieppe ground. Latter half of the 18th century. From the M. Wuyts Collection, Wijnegem, Belgium. Photo: t' Felt, Antwerp.*

16 *Detail of a Mechlin bobbin lace, Drochel ground.*
First half of the 19th century. From the M. Wuyts
Collection, Wijnegem, Belgium. Photo: t' Felt,
Antwerp.

42

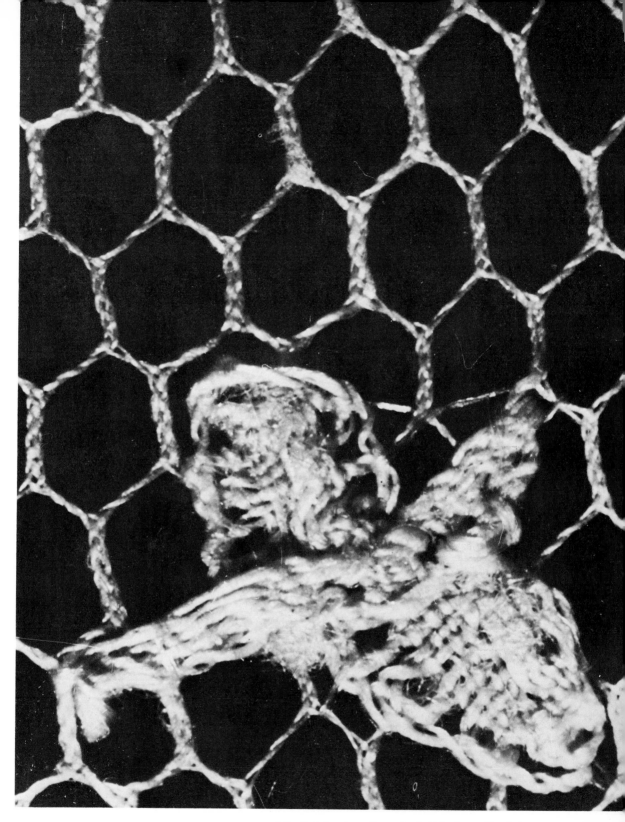

17 Detail of a Brussels bobbin lace, Drochel ground. About 1810–1820. From the M. Wuyts Collection, Wijnegem, Belgium. Photo: t' Felt, Antwerp.

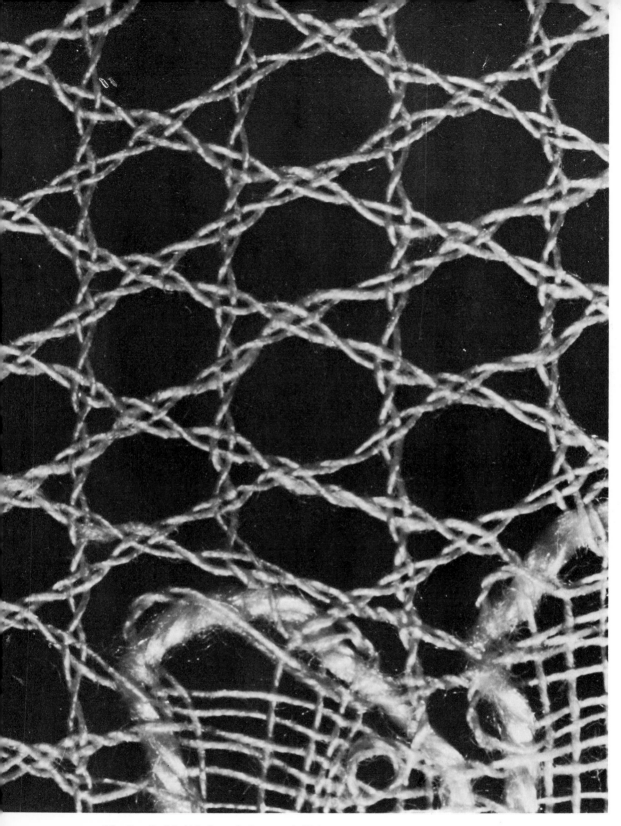

18   Detail of bobbin lace, Paris ground. 20th century. Collection of Mej. M. van Hamme, Antwerp.
Photo: t' Felt, Antwerp.

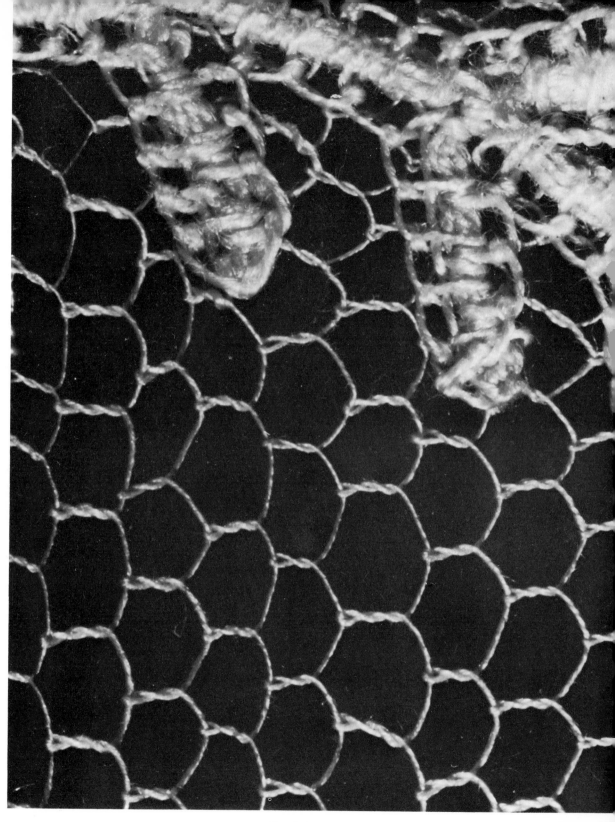

19   Point d'Angleterre with double tulle, Huis Galle,
Antwerp, 20th century. Brussels bobbin lace is
combined with needlepoint. From the M. van Hamme
Collection. Photo: t' Felt, Antwerp.

45

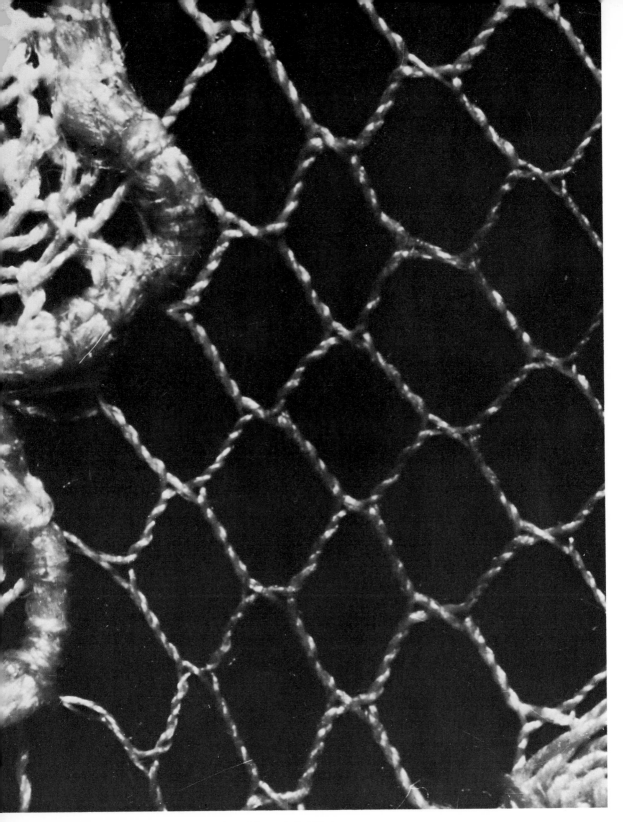

20   Detail of an application of Brussels bobbin lace
to net. About 1880. From the M. Wuyts Collection,
Wijnegem, Belgium. Photo: t' Felt, Antwerp.

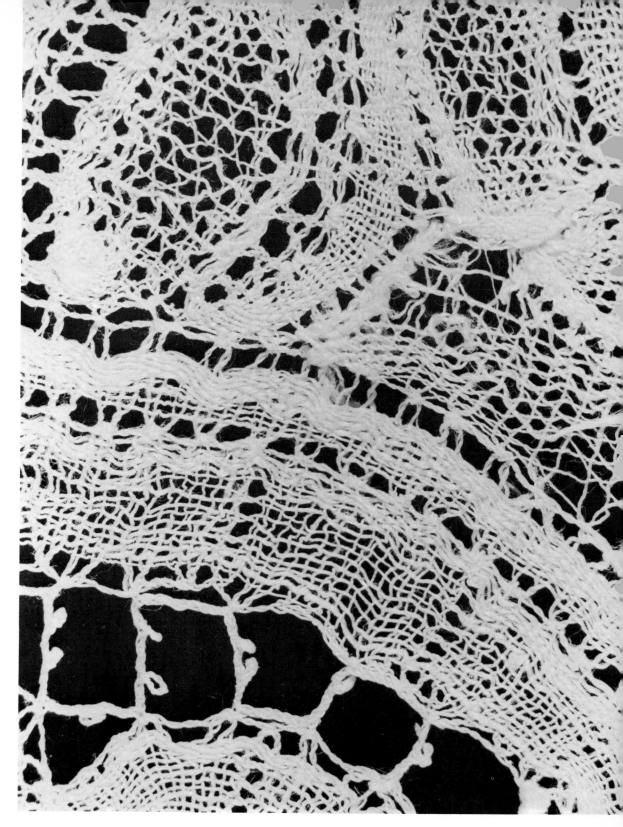

21 Detail of Brussels bobbin lace with blond, cloth stitch and half-stitch. Early 18th century. From the Sterckshof Museum, Deurne-Antwerp. Photo: t' Felt, Antwerp.

47

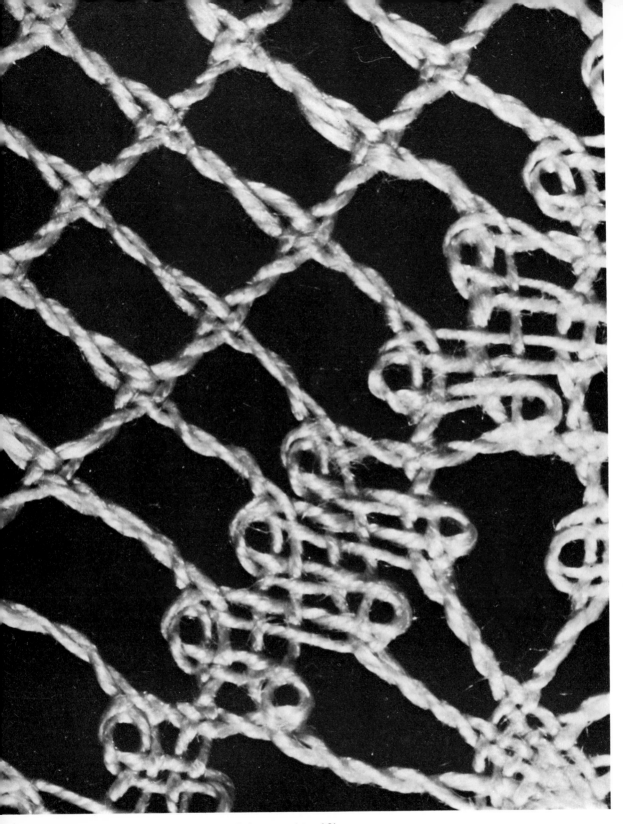

22 *Detail of a bobbin-made lace, a variety of Cluny*
lace. 20th century. From the M. Wuyts Collection,
Wijnegem, Belgium. Photo: t' Felt, Antwerp.

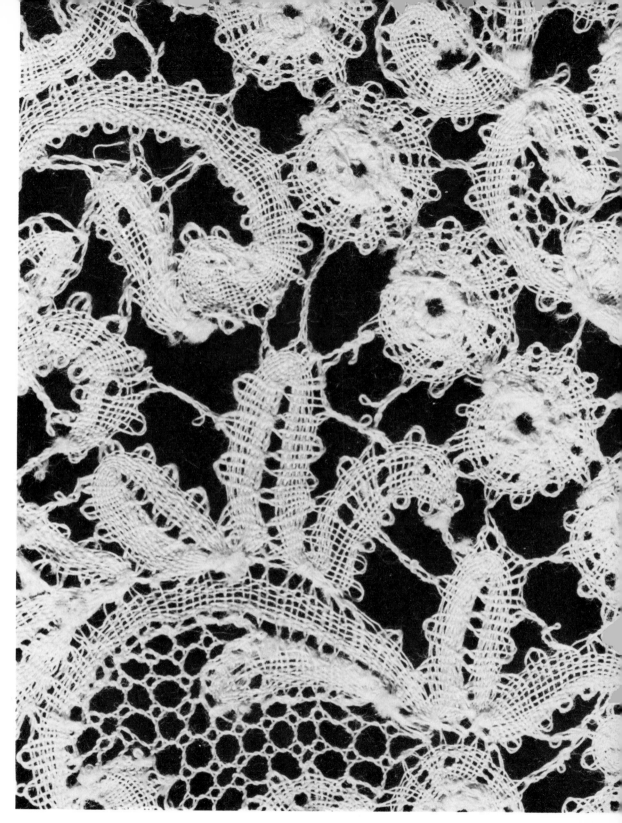

23 Detail of a bobbin lace tablecloth in rosaline perlée, about 1925. Photo: t' Felt, Antwerp.

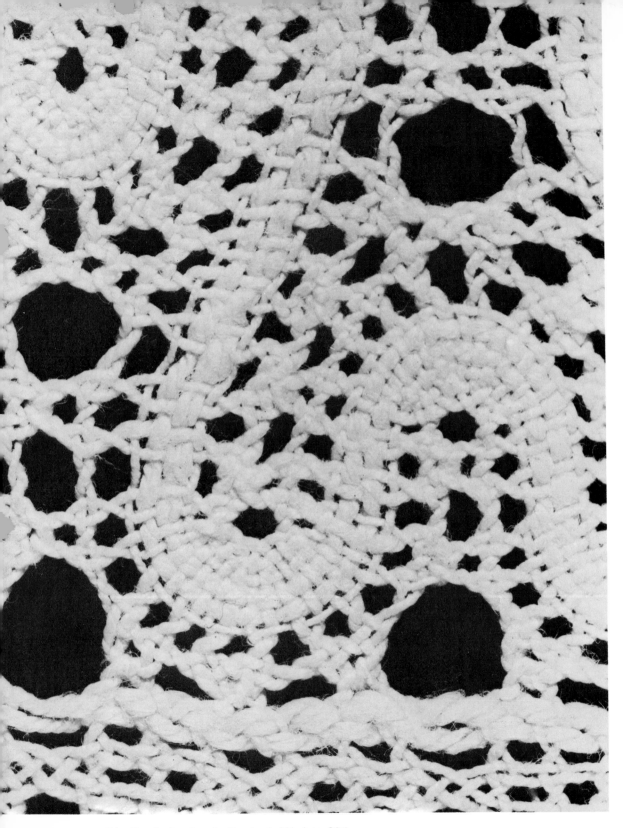

24   Detail of centre of a Russian bobbin lace, 20th
century. From M. Wuyts Collection, Wijnegem,
Belgium. Photo: t' Felt, Antwerp.

25 Detail of a bobbin lace bedspread presented by the municipality of Brussels to the Archduke Albert of Flanders and his bride Isabella, on the occasion of their marriage, 1599. By courtesy of the Royal Museums of Art and History, Brussels.

25A   *Further details from the Brussels bedspread.*

25B *Further details from the Brussels bedspread.*

26 Needlepoint, 1911, with a very rare type of ground on the bust. Size of the original motif is 36×27 cm (about $14 \times 10\frac{1}{2}$ in). From the M. Wuyts Collection, Wijnegem, Belgium. Photo: Wuyts.

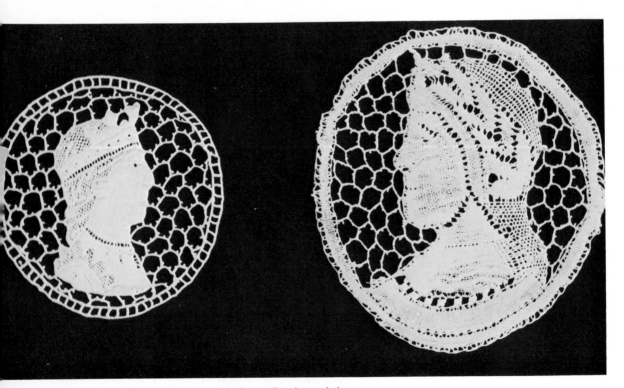

27 The left-hand motif is in needlepoint and the right-hand one in bobbin lace. Diameters 10 cm (4 in) and 13·5 cm ($5\frac{1}{2}$ in.) respectively. From the M. Wuyts Collection, Wijnegem, Belgium.

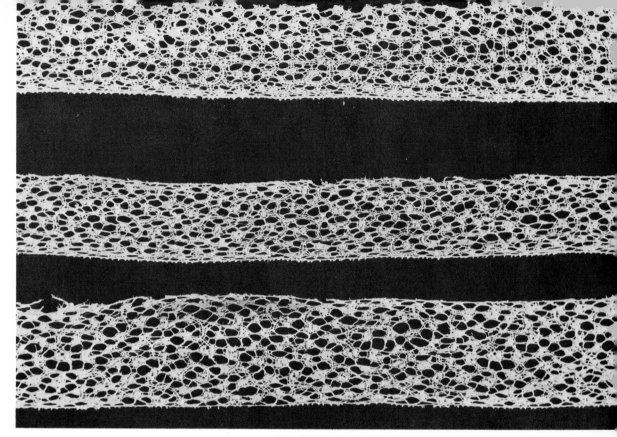

28 Three insertions of so-called "old Flemish" lace, probably made without a pattern. 6 × 64 cm (about 2½ × 25 in). 17th century. From the M. Wuyts Collection, Wijnegem, Belgium.

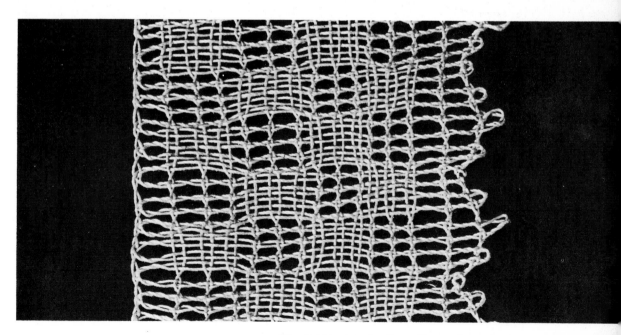

29 Bobbin lace by Grete Thums, Brno, Czecho-slovakia. About 1930. Width 3·8 cm (about 1½ in). By courtesy of the State Museum of Applied Art, Munich (New Collection).

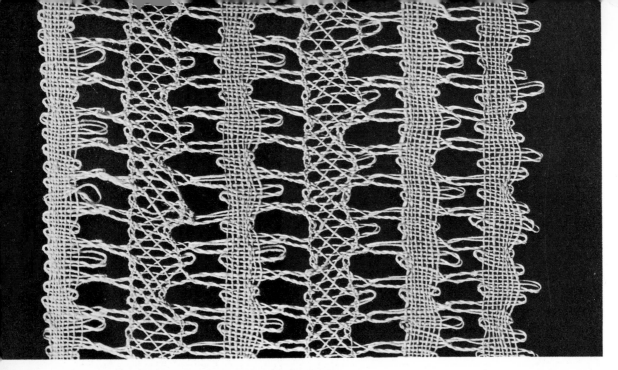

30 Bobbin lace by Grete Thums, Brno, Czecho-
slovakia. Width 7·8 cm (3 in). By courtesy of the
State Museum of Applied Art, Munich (New
Collection).

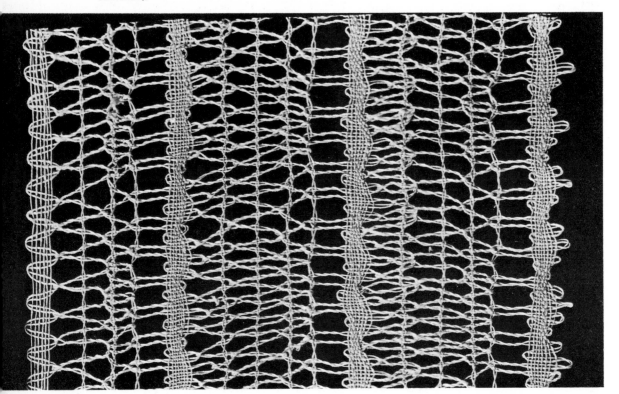

31 Bobbin lace by Grete Thums. Width 9·6 cm
(about 3½ in). By courtesy of the State Museum of
Applied Art, Munich (New Collection).

32 Bobbin lace, torchon designs, designed and executed by Professor Gerhard Kadow, Krefeld, Germany, 1951. Width 14 cm (5½ in).

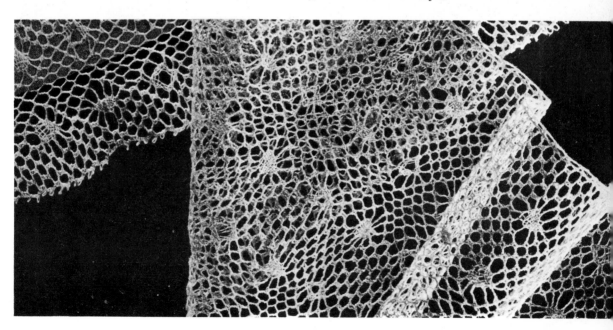

33 Bobbin lace designed and executed by Professor Gerhard Kadow, Krefeld, Germany. 1952. Width 14 cm (5½ in).

33A Bobbin lace designed and executed by Professor Gerhard Kadow, Krefeld, Germany.

33B Bobbin lace designed and executed by Professor Gerhard Kadow, Krefeld, Germany. 1972 and 1973.

58

34 Detail of "duchesse" lace, in which some
bobbin lace motifs have been assembled by means
of the needle. About 1880. 10 × 45 cm (about
4 × 17¾ in). From the M. Wuyts Collection, Wijnegem,
Belgium.

36 Teneriffe lace. Linen. 36 × 36 cm (about 14¼ in
square). 20th century. From the M. Wuyts Collection,
Wijnegem, Belgium.

35 Enlarged detail of Teneriffe lace made on a "wheel" in linen thread. 36 × 36 cm (about 14¼ in square). 20th century. From the M. Wuyts Collection, Wijnegem, Belgium.

37 A lace patchwork assembled in 1930. It consists of 20 putti in filet lace, 68 pieces of needlepoint of Venetian origin, and a bobbin lace border in Venetian style, with some other pieces of point lace. From the M. Wuyts Collection, Wijnegem, Belgium.

38 Some more details from the previous piece.

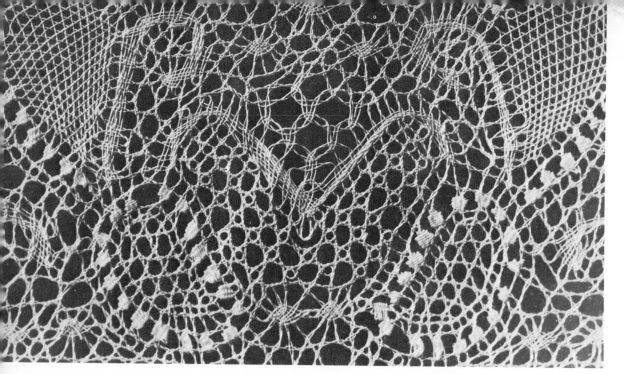

39 Binche bobbin lace, 23 × 23 cm (about 9 in square). Bruges, 20th century. Technically it seems to be a modern development of the old Flemish Binche lace that was made in the first half of the 18th century. Mej. M. van Hamme Collection, Antwerp.

40 Two border laces from Halas, Hungary, de-
41 signed by Arpad Dekani, 1906. Needlepoint in multi-coloured silks. The upper border is 7 cm (2¾ in) deep, the lower 10 cm (4 in). Museum of Arts and Crafts, Budapest.

42 Hunnia (Hungary) lace border, needlepoint in white linen thread, 1906. 5 cm (about 2 in) deep. Museum of Arts and Crafts, Budapest.

43 Detail of a coverlet in needlepoint, bobbin and filet lace, designed by M. Mezzara, Paris. Decorative Art Museum, Paris.

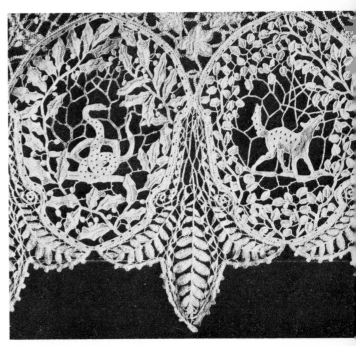

44 A further detail of the Mezzara coverlet.

45 *Four original sketches by Dagobert Peche for*

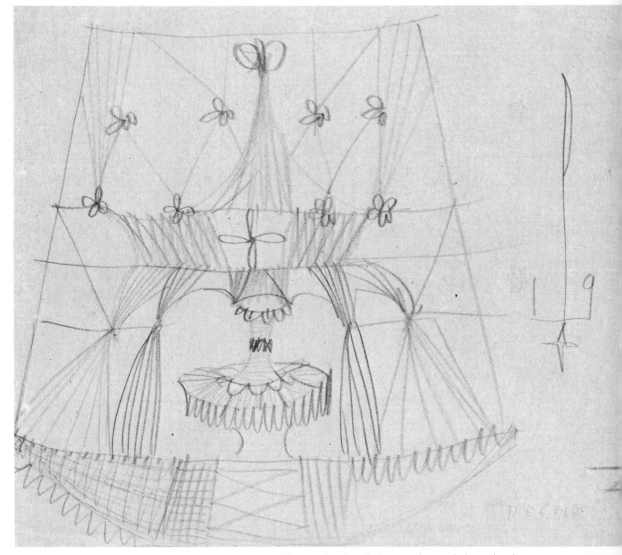

46 needlepoint designs to be carried out by the
Vienna Workshops. 1916. Property of the author.
(Continued overleaf).   65

47, 48   See previous page.

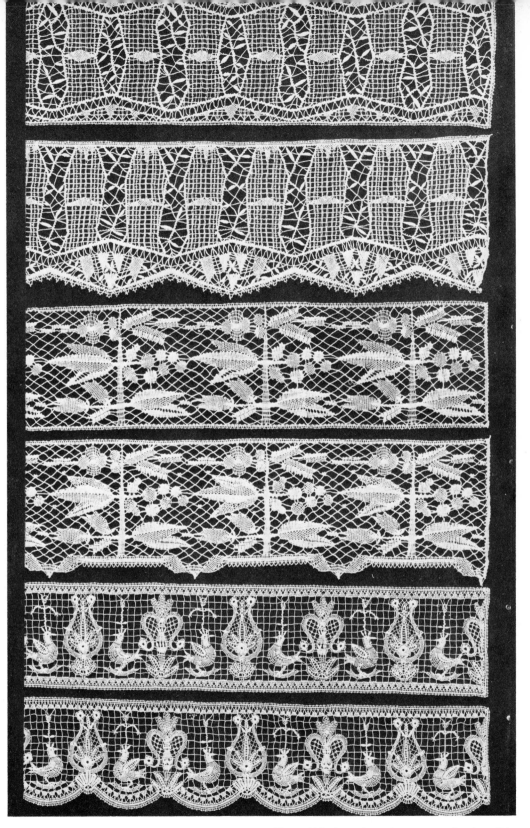

49 Bobbin laces from the pattern collection of the Vienna Workshops, about 1920.

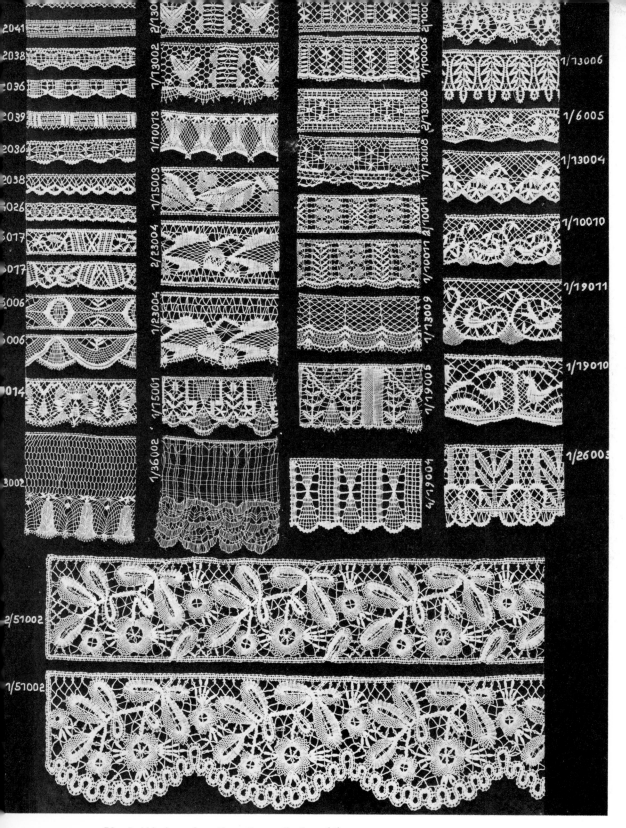

50   Bobbin laces from the pattern collection of the
Vienna Workshops, about 1920.

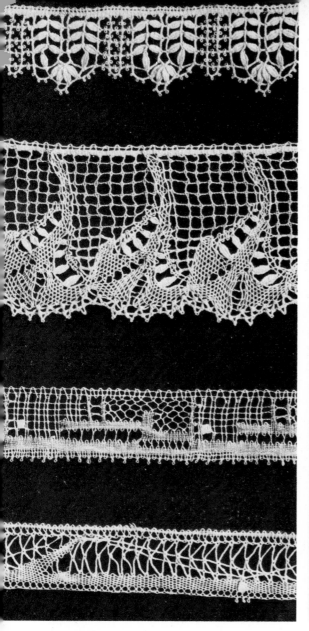

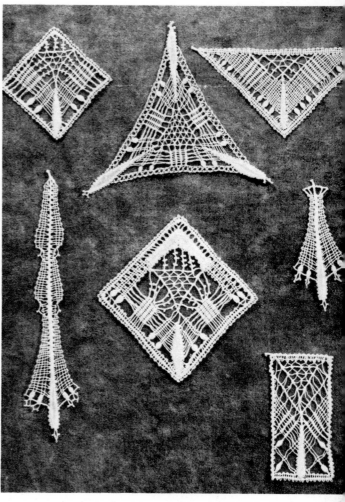

51 Bobbin laces designed and executed 1911–
1914 by Leni Matthaei, Reutlingen, Germany. Photo:
Dr. Knoefel.

52 Bobbin laces designed and executed by Leni
Matthaei. The motifs (photo: Renger-Patzsch) were
designed in 1915 and the insertions (photo: Hein
Gorny) between 1918 and 1924.

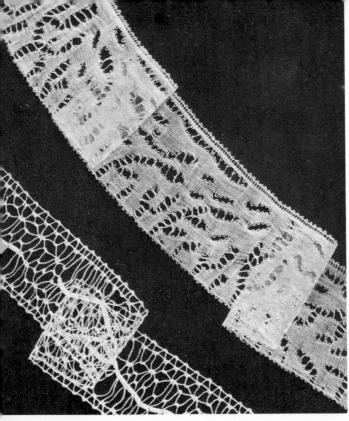

53   Further bobbin laces by Leni Matthaei.

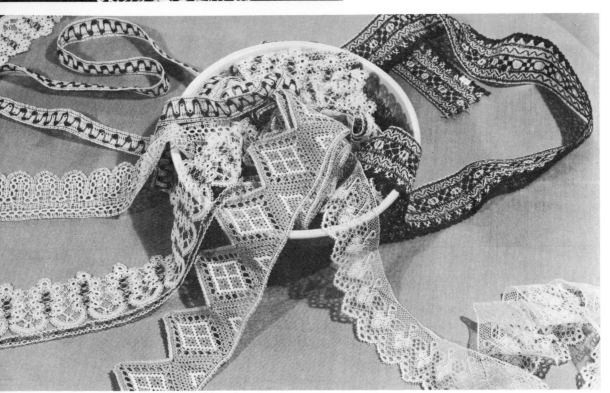

54   Bobbin laces including the use of colour, made as part of Slovak national costume. From the Co-operative for the Production of Folk Art, Bratislava. Photo: Deutsche Fotothek, Dresden.

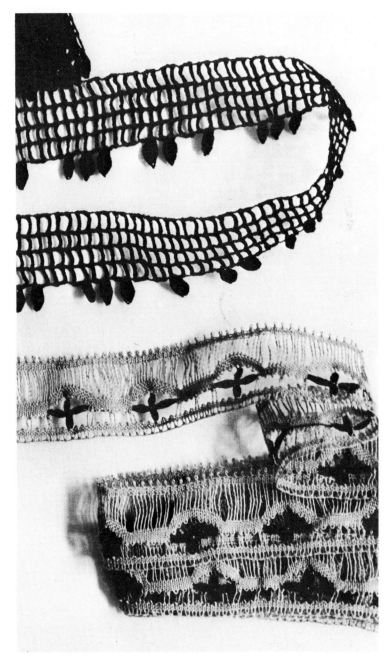

55 Coloured bobbin laces. Designed by Suse
Bernuth, Wuppertal, Germany, and executed by the
State School of Bobbin Lace, Tiefenbach, 1954–
1962. By courtesy of the Museum of Applied Art
(New Collection) Munich. Photo: Adolf Hierzegger,
Berchtesgaden.

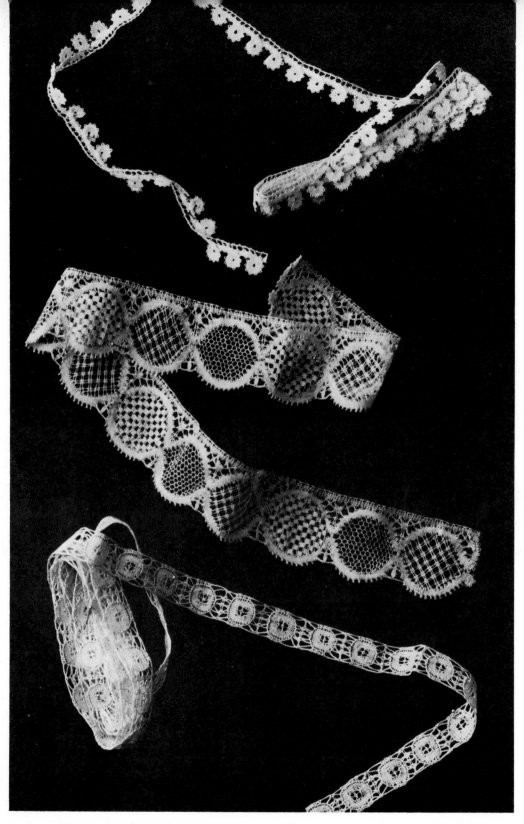

56 Bobbin laces designed by Suse Bernuth, Wuppertal, Germany. Top: braid in linen thread. Centre: edging with clothstitch braid circles, with fillings in Brussels ground, Torchon squares and Lattice. Bottom: cloth stitch with purl. Executed by the State School of Bobbin Lace, Tiefenbach, Germany. By courtesy of the Institute for the Advancement of Crafts, Stuttgart. Photo: Adolf Hierzegger, Berchtesgaden. 1954–1962.

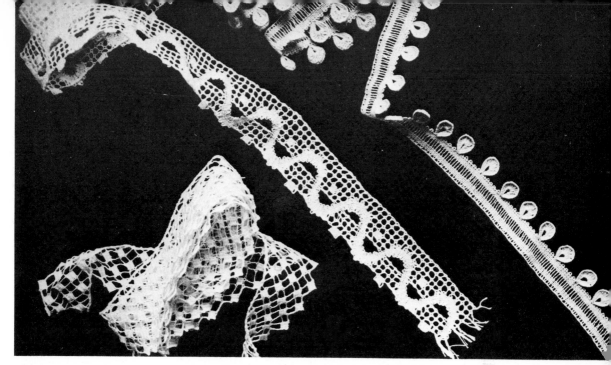

57 Bobbin lace designed by Suse Bernuth, Wuppertal, and executed by the State School of Bobbin Lace, Tiefenbach, Germany, 1954–1962. By courtesy of the Museum of Applied Art (New Collection), Munich. Photo: Adolf Hierzegger, Berchtesgaden.

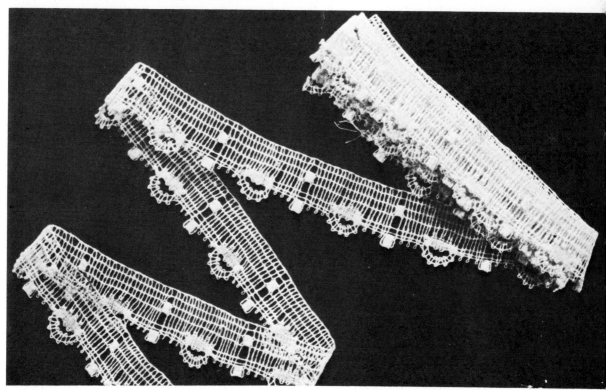

58 Bobbin lace designed by Suse Bernuth, Wuppertal, and executed by the State School of Bobbin Lace, Schönsee, Germany, 1954–1962. By courtesy of the Museum of Applied Art (New Collection), Munich. Photo: Adolf Hierzegger, Berchtesgaden.

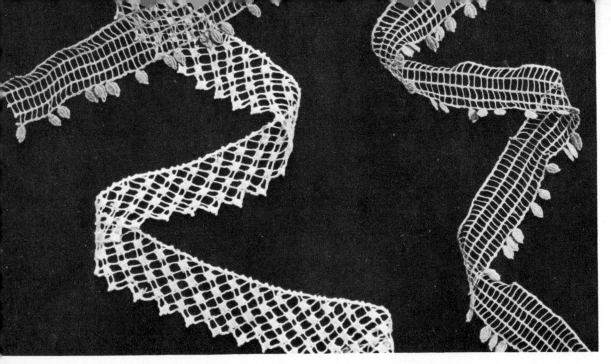

59 Bobbin laces designed by Suse Bernuth, Wuppertal, 1960. Executed in the State School of Bobbin Lace, Tiefenbach, Germany. Property of the Museum of Applied Art (New Collection), Munich.

Photo: Adolf Hierzegger, Berchtesgaden.

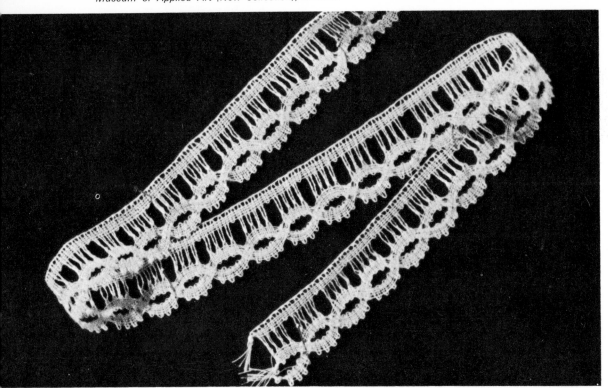

60 Bobbin lace designed by Suse Bernuth, Wuppertal. Executed by the State School of Bobbin Lace, Schönsee, Germany, 1954–1962. By courtesy of the Museum of Applied Art (New Collection),

Munich. Photo: Adolf Hierzegger, Berchtesgaden.

61 Bobbin lace designed by Suse Bernuth, Wuppertal. Executed by the State School of Bobbin Lace, Schönsee, Germany, 1954–1962. Institute of Advancement of Crafts, Stuttgart. Photo: Adolf Hierzegger, Berchtesgaden.

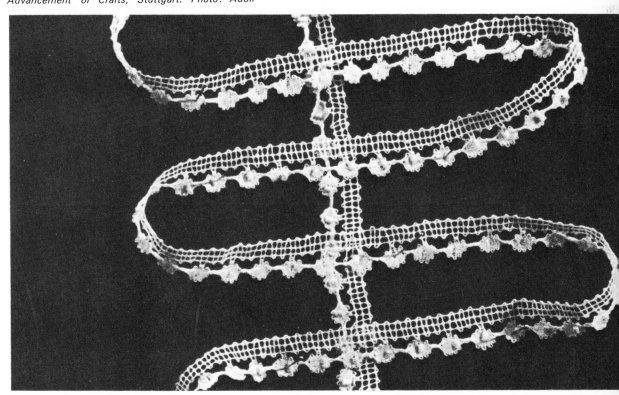

62 Bobbin lace designed by Suse Bernuth, Wuppertal, 1954–1962. Executed by the State School of Bobbin Lace, Schönsee, Germany. Photo: Adolf Hierzegger, Berchtesgaden.

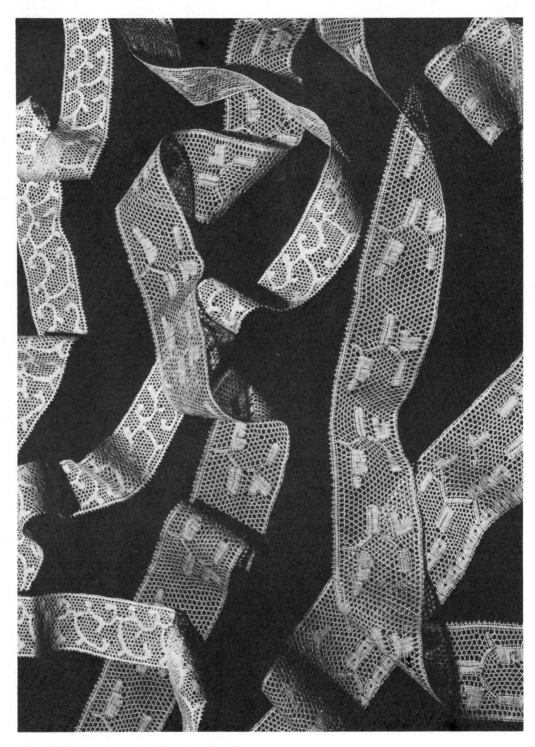

63 Bobbin insertion and edging laces from Cogne
and Fobello, Aosta, Italy. 1940. By courtesy of the
Emma Sichart Lace Archive, Munich, Germany.

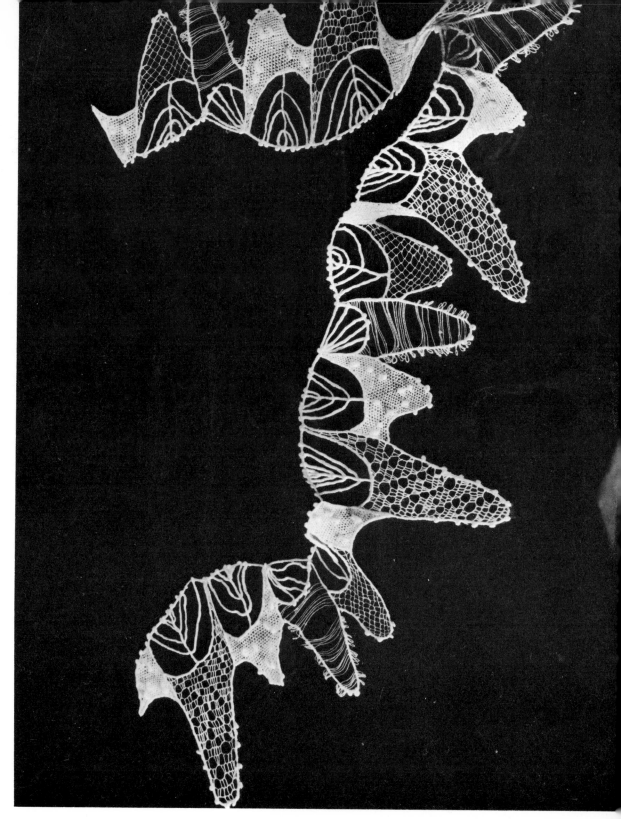

64 *"Pointed arches", needle-made lace. Designed and executed by Professor Hanne-Nüte Kämmerer, Detmold, Germany, 1955. Photo: Pan Walther, Münster*

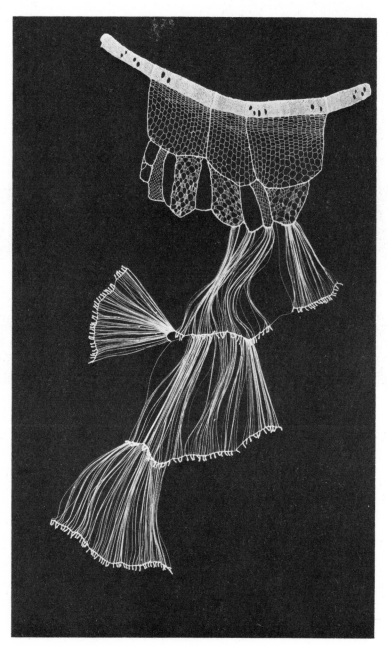

65 *"Opening blossoms", needle-made lace. De-*
signed and executed by Professor Hanne-Nüte
Kämmerer, Detmold, Germany, 1962. By courtesy
of the Museum of Arts and Crafts, Cologne.
30 × 17 cm (about 12 × 6¾ in). Photo: Wölbing
van Dyck, Bielefeld.

66 "Lacy ladder", needlepoint lace. Designed and executed by Professor Hanne-Nüte Kämmerer, Detmold, Germany, 1956. Photo: Pan Walther, Münster. Property of the artist.

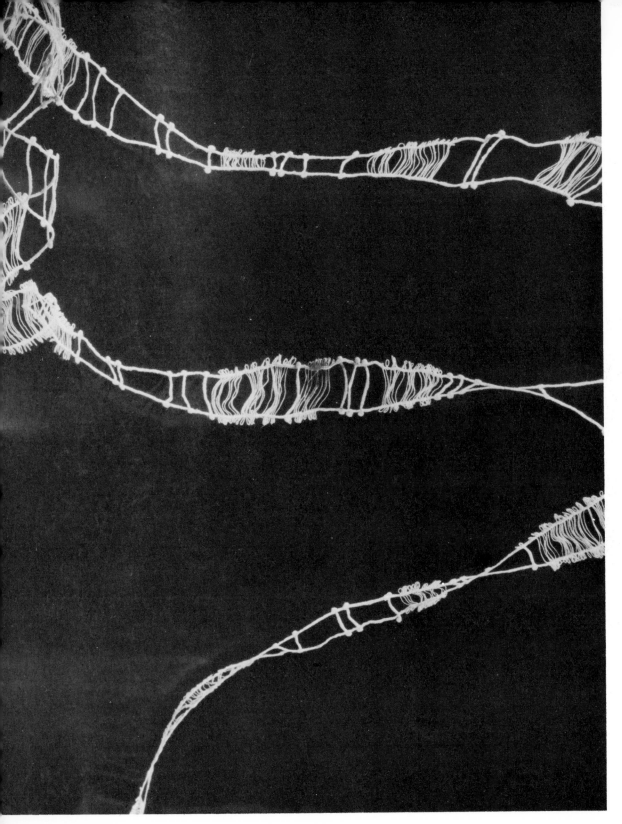

67 *"Narrow ladder" needlepoint lace. Designed and executed by Professor Hanne-Nüte Kämmerer, Detmold, Germany, 1956. Photo: Pan Walther, Münster. Property of the artist.*

68 Bobbin lace border, designed and executed by Grete Thums, Brno, Czechoslovakia.

69 Bobbin lace curtain with a motif of poultry. Cream-coloured, with foliage in yellow, pink and green. A single panel measures $2 \cdot 50 \times 0 \cdot 75$ m (about 98×30 in). Each motif is 40 cm wide $\times$ 45 cm high (about $15\frac{1}{4} \times 17\frac{1}{2}$ in). Folk Art Centre, Moscow. Produced by the Vologa District Co-operative. Photo: Deutsche Fotothek (Kramer), Dresden.

70 Bobbin lace mat in blue and white. Designed
by Suse Bernuth, Wuppertal, Germany. Executed
by the State School of Bobbin Lace, Tiefenbach,
Germany, 1952–1964. Property of Frau Fann
Schniewind, Wuppertal. Photo: Abel-Menne,
Wuppertal.

71 Bobbin lace tablecloth in blue, white and pink.
Designed by Suse Bernuth, Wuppertal, Germany.
Executed by the State School of Bobbin Lace,
Tiefenbach, 1952–1964. Photo: Hierzegger-Foto,
Berchtesgaden.

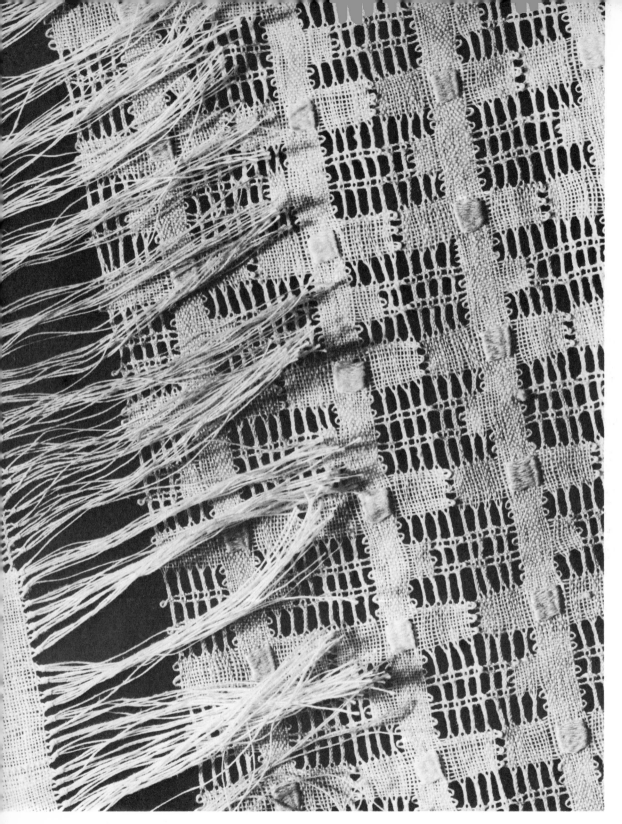

72 Tablecloth in unbleached and white linen.
Designed by Suse Bernuth, Wuppertal, Germany.
Executed by the State School of Bobbin Lace,
Tiefenbach, Germany, 1952–1964. Photo: Abel-
Menne, Wuppertal.

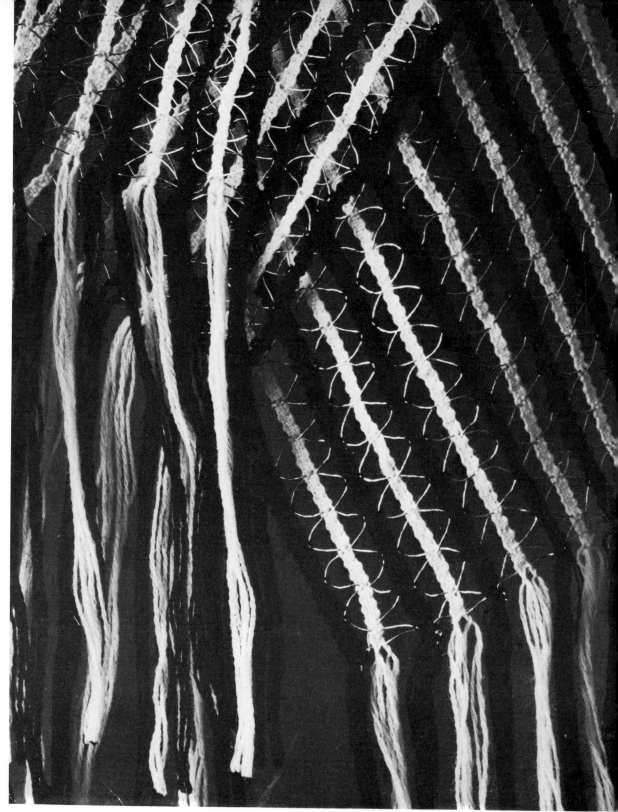

73 Bobbin lace stole in wool with gold Lurex.
2 m long × 90 cm wide (78 × 35½ in approximately).
Designed by Suse Bernuth, Wuppertal, Germany.
Executed by the State School of Bobbin Lace,
Schönsee, Germany, 1954–1962.

85

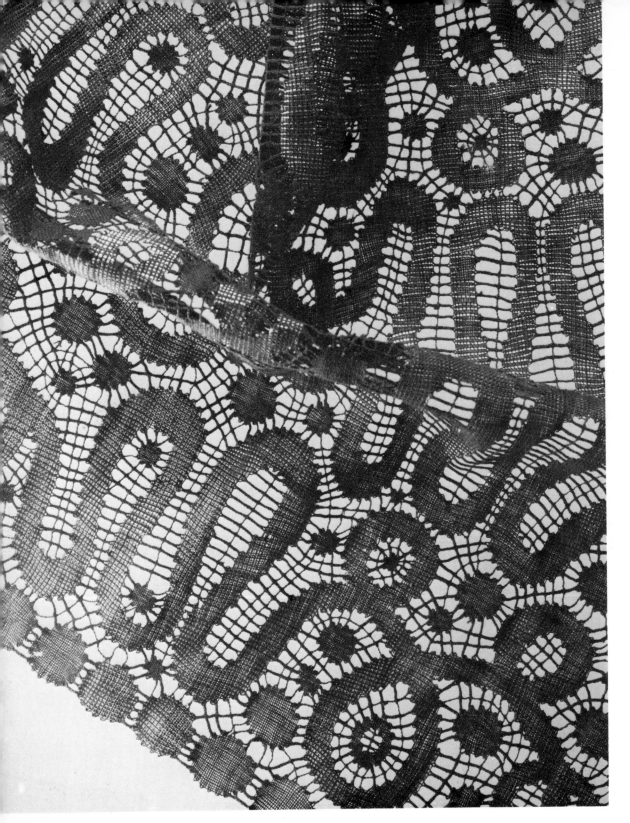

74 Bobbin lace fabric in violet with gold Lurex.
Designed by Suse Bernuth, Wuppertal, Germany.
Executed by the State School of Bobbin Lace,
Tiefenbach, Germany, 1954–1962. Proprietor: Frau
Fann Schniewind, Wuppertal. Photo: Abel-Menne,
Wuppertal.

75 Bobbin lace stole, gold Lurex and black linen.
1·20 × 2·50 m (about 47 × 98 in). Designed by Suse
Bernuth, Wuppertal, Germany. Executed by the State
School of Bobbin Lace, Tiefenbach, Germany, 1954–
1962. Photo: Abel-Menne, Wuppertal. Proprietor:
Frau Fann Schiewind, Wuppertal.

76 Bobbin lace strip, 15 cm (about 6 in) wide,
black with gold Lurex. Designed by Suse Bernuth,
Wuppertal, Germany. Executed by the State School
of Bobbin Lace, Tiefenbach, Germany, 1954–1962.
Photo: Abel-Menne, Wuppertal.

77 Stole with bobbin lace. Designed by Suse Bernuth, Wuppertal, Germany. Executed by the Bobbin Lace School in Stadlern, Germany, 1954–1962. Photo: Abel-Menne, Wuppertal. Proprietor: Institute for the Advancement of Crafts, Stuttgart.

78   Bobbin lace duchess set, Italian, about 1930.
Photo: Fabbri, Rome.

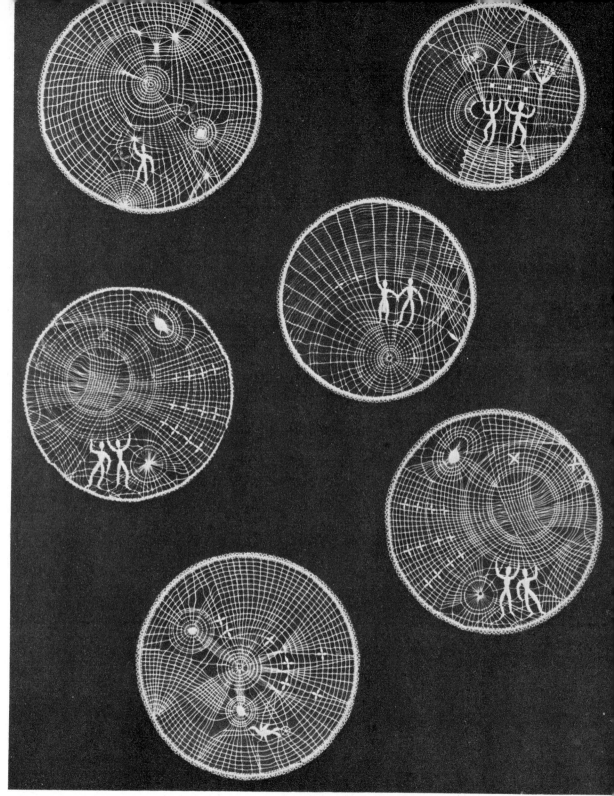

79   *Coverlet by Emilie Palicková, reproduced from*
Emilie Palicková by Ludmilla Kybalová, Czech Pub-
lishing House for the Fine Arts, Prague, 1962. The   91
coverlet was made in 1940–1945.

80 Embroidery on tulle, designed by Dagobert
Peche, 1924. Executed by the Vienna Workshops.

"Chevron", 1.5 x 0.91 metres (5 x 3 feet).
Mohair and wool. 1971.Sherri Smith, U.S.A.

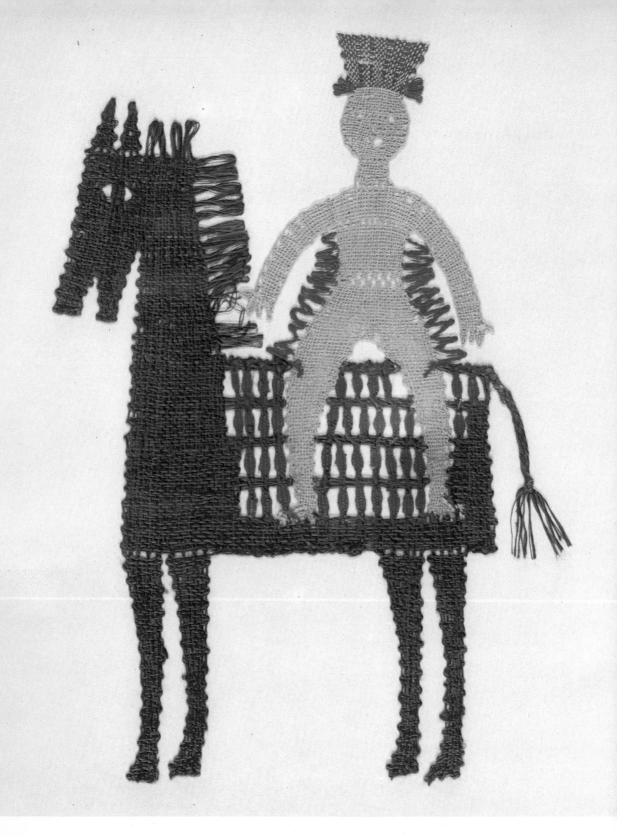

*"Horse and Rider", 26 x 18 cm (10¼ x 7½ in), by
Hana Králová, Czechoslovakia, about 1960.*

81   Tea-table cloth, embroidered tulle: "Stories and legends of Lower Saxony". Designed and executed by Anna Gehring, Hameln, Germany. Photo: Curt Bieling, Berlin. Reproduced from Handarbeiten Aller Art, 1942.

82   Detail from cloth in embroidered tulle: "Stories
and Legends of Hameln". Designed and executed by
Anna Gehring. The town is better known to English
readers as the Hamelin of The Pied Piper: "Hamelin
town's in Brunswick, By famous Hanover city. . . ."

83 Shawl in black needlepoint lace, Venetian
style, 1939. Designed by Professor Dante Sernesi.
From the Istituto Statale d'Arte, Cantu, Como, Italy.   95

84 Tablecloth, diameter 93·95 cm (about 37 in)
with 30 bobbin lace scrolls. Designed and worked
by Leni Matthaei, Reutlingen, Germany. The basic
design was created in 1911. The tablecloth, made
in handspun linen, was exhibited in 1973. Photo:
Uhland-Clauss, Esslingen.

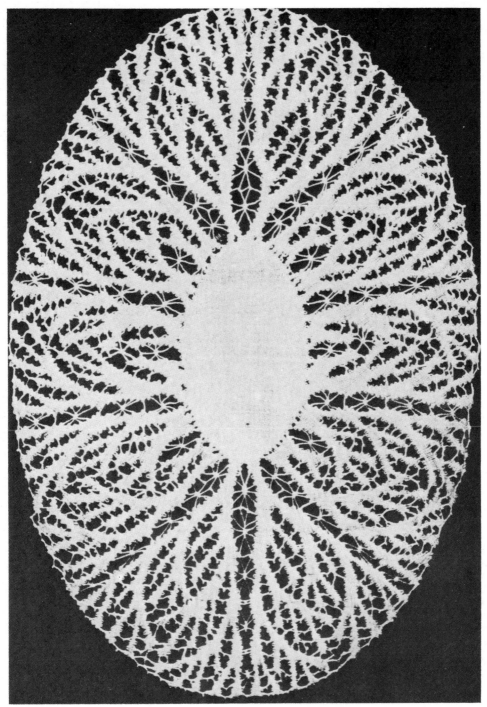

85   ''Coral''. Bobbin lace, 22 × 30 cm (8¾ × 12 in),
designed and executed by Leni Matthaei, Reutlingen,
Germany, 1906–1907.   97

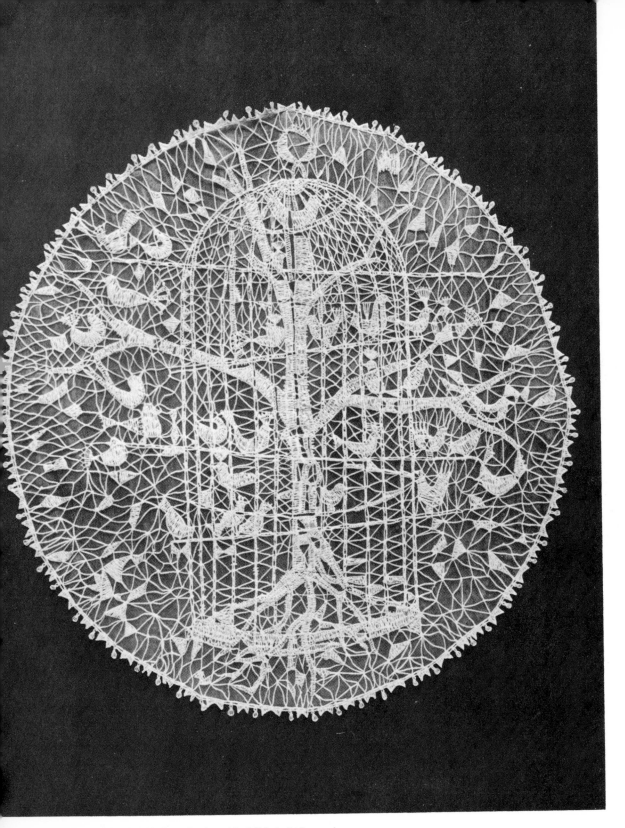

86   Bobbin lace. Designed by Michela Di Domenico
Fegarotti, executed by Leda Fatti, Sansepolcro, Italy.

87 Filet lace from the lace factory at Bosa. ENAPI
Sardinia.

88   Bobbin lace by Franca, Gorizia, Italy.

89 *Bobbin lace designed by Mario Giampieri,*
executed by Genoeffa Molteni & Sons, Cantu, Italy.

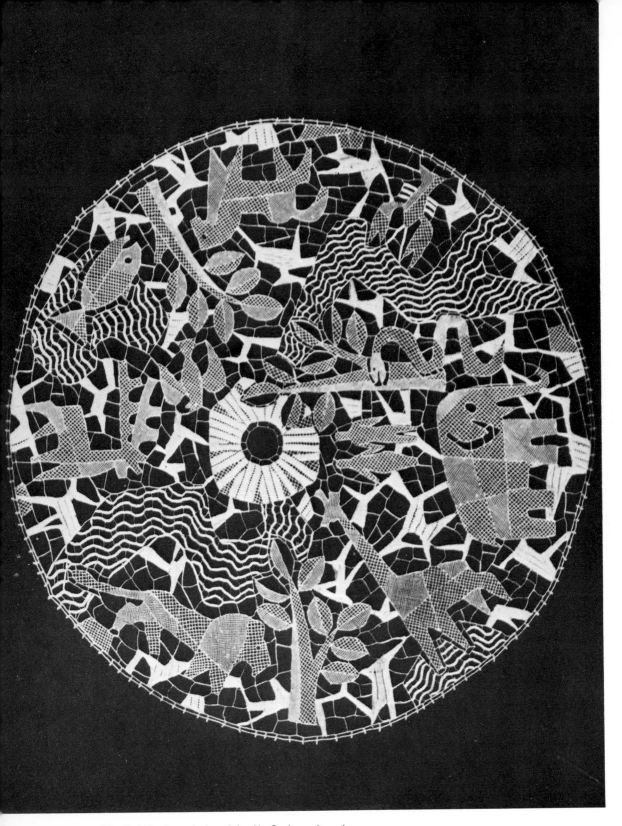

90 *Bobbin lace designed by H. Gschwendt and executed by Rosa Mittermair at the School of Lace, Predoi, Adige, Italy.*

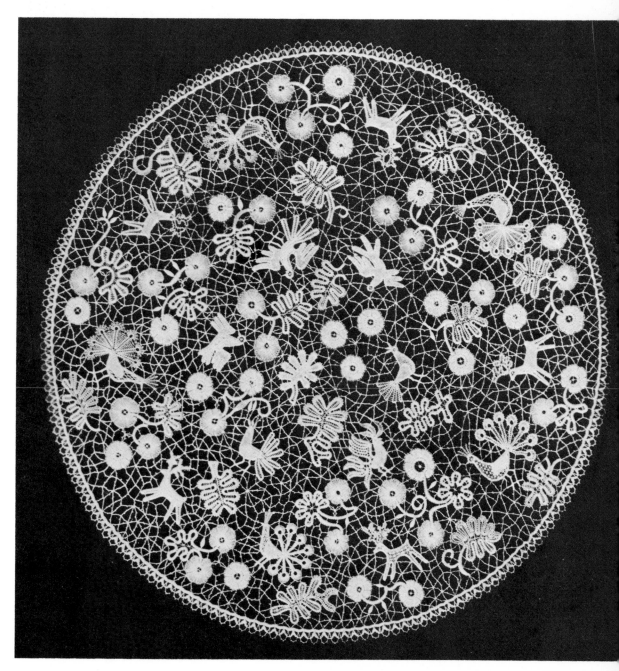

91 Bobbin lace designed by Guglielmo Riavis, executed at the State School of Lace, Gorizia, Italy.

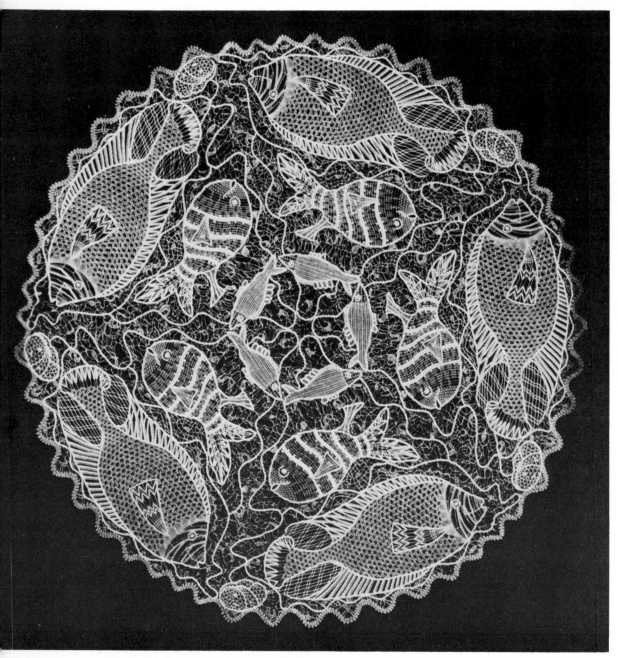

92   Bobbin lace designed by Helga Erhall, executed
by Hilda Duregger at the School of Lace, Predoi,
Valle Aurina, Italy.

93 Bobbin lace, designed by Romualdo Scarpa and Serena Del Maschio, executed by Jesurum, Venice.

94 Bobbin Lace, designed by Leonardo Spreafico, executed by Giulio Galbiati and Sons, Cantù, Italy.

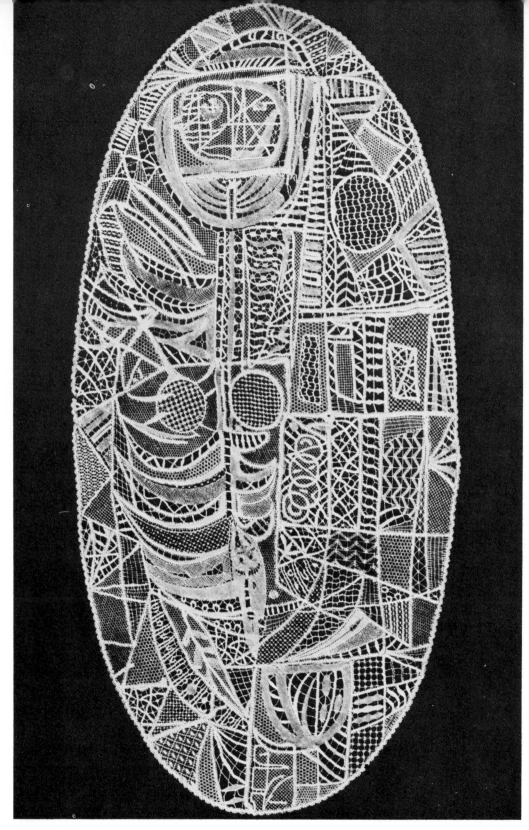

95 Bobbin lace designed by Leonardo Spreafico,
executed by Manifatture Riunite Merletti at Cantù,
Italy.

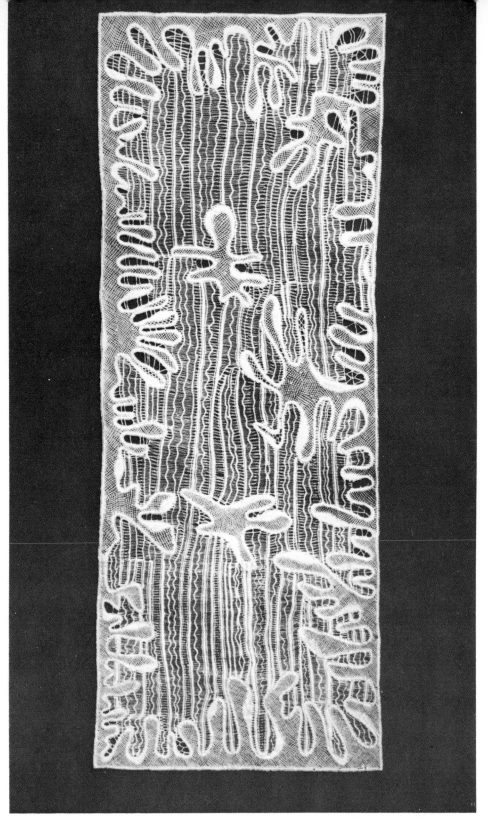

96 *Bobbin lace designed by Leonardo Spreafico,*
executed by Manifatture Riunite Merletti at Cantù,
Italy.   107

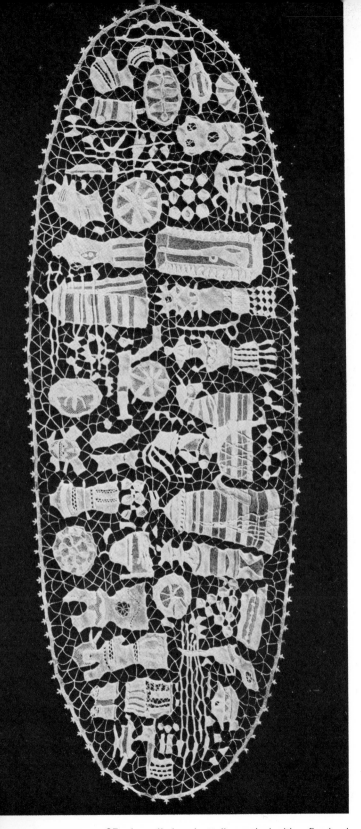

97 Lace ''ad uncinetto''—worked with a fine hook
—designed by Michela Di Domenico Fegarotti,
executed by Ars Wetana, Orvieto, Italy.

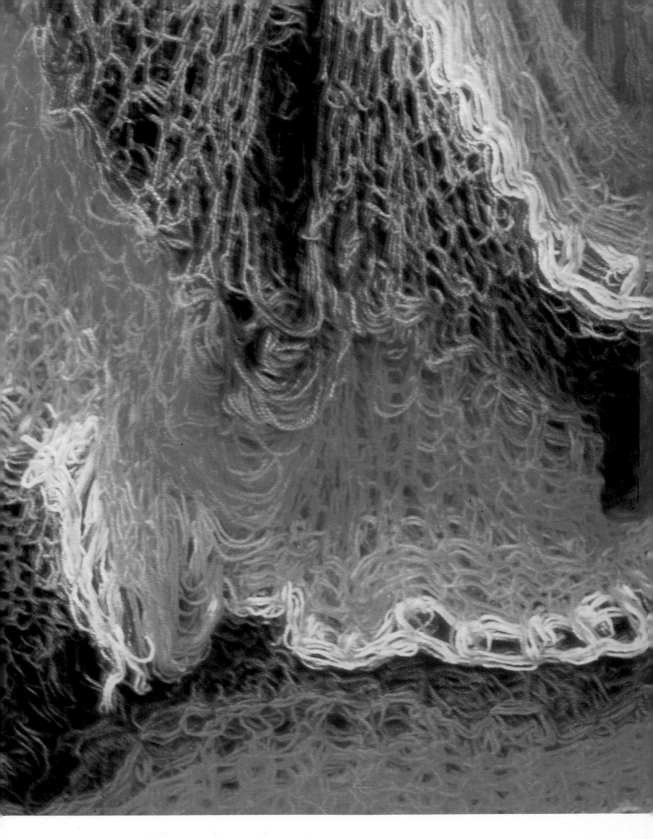

"Rainbow Conch", 1.8 x 1.2 x 1.2 metres (6 x 4
x 4 feet). Wool, 1973. Sherri Smith, U.S.A.

Circular weaving using lace technique, designed and executed by Hedwig Klöckner-Triebe, Münster, Germany. Linen with beads, 12.7 x 14.2 cm (about 5 x 5¾ in).

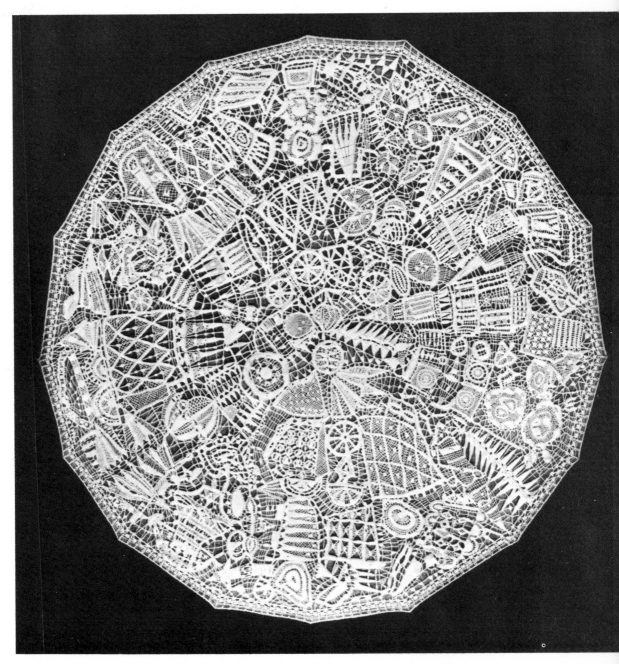

98 Bobbin lace designed by Eugenio Fegarotti,
executed by Leda Fatti, Sansepolcro, Italy.

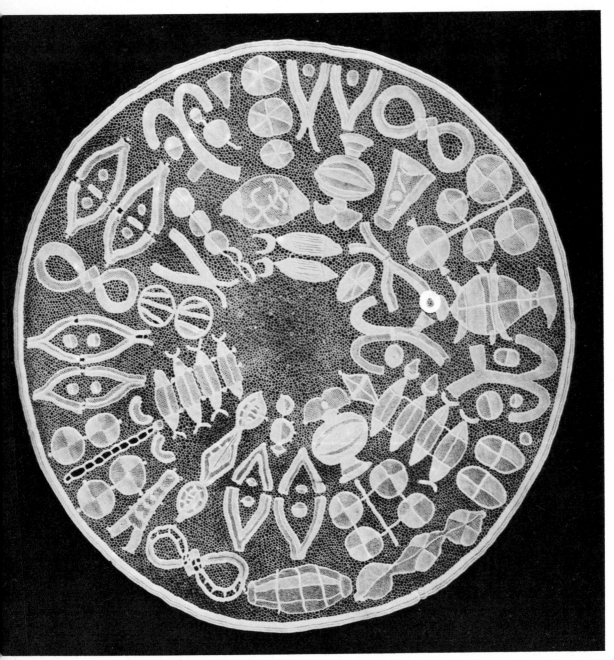

99 Lace, "ad uncinetto", designed by Eugenio
Fegarotti, executed by Ars Wetana, Orvieto, Italy.

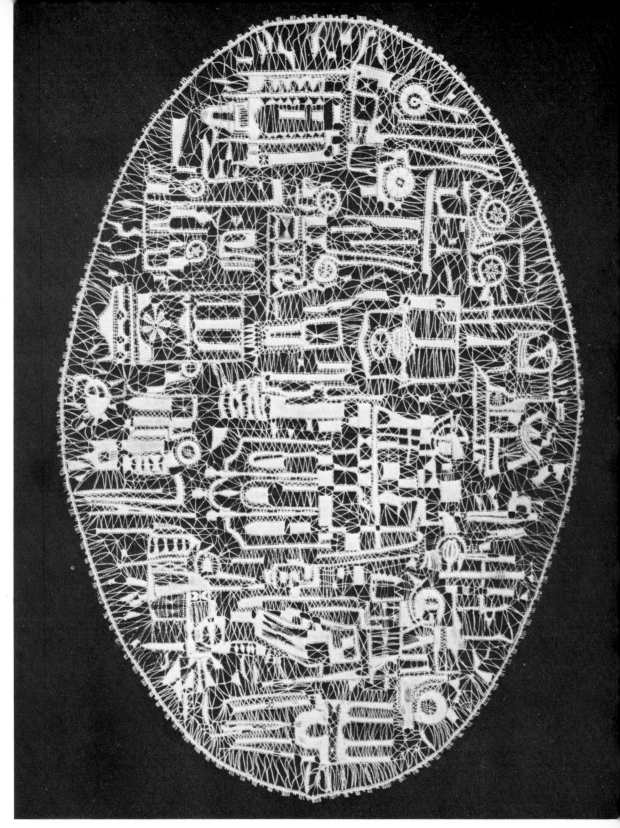

100   Bobbin lace designed by Michela Di Domenico
Fegarotti, executed by Gina Brizzi, Arezzo, Italy.

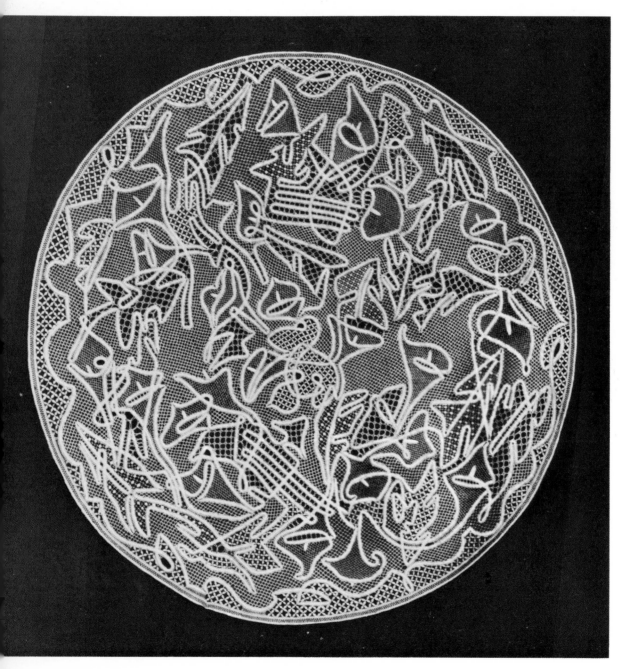

101 Bobbin lace designed by Vando Tapparini,
executed by Maria Tollis of the School of Bobbin
Lace, Pecocostanzo, Italy.

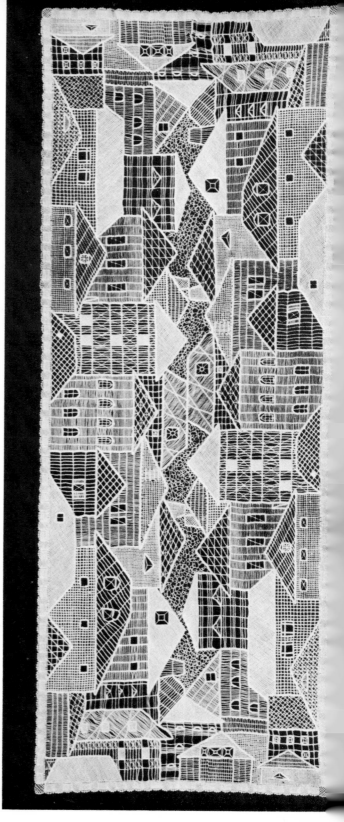

102 "The Little City"—bobbin lace designed by
Helga Ehall, executed by Luigia Mittermair at the
School of Lace, Predoi, Valle Aurina, Italy.

The photographs in this group, from 103 to 108, were supplied by Mrs Sybil Allan, and the photographer was Reginald Frost, FIIP, FRPS. The coin shown in some of them, to give scale, is an English 5p piece, about the size of the US nickel. (Diameter just under 2·5 cm or 1 in.)

103   Cloth for a coffee-table worked by Mrs Doris Bird from an Italian pattern, using 154 bobbins and No. 80 linen thread. Mrs Bird is a native of Bedfordshire who took up lace-making in Sheffield in 1966.

104   Dress ornament adapted from a Bruges design by Mrs Edna Taylor, who was introduced to lace-making through the Townswomen's Guild and now teaches her own private group.

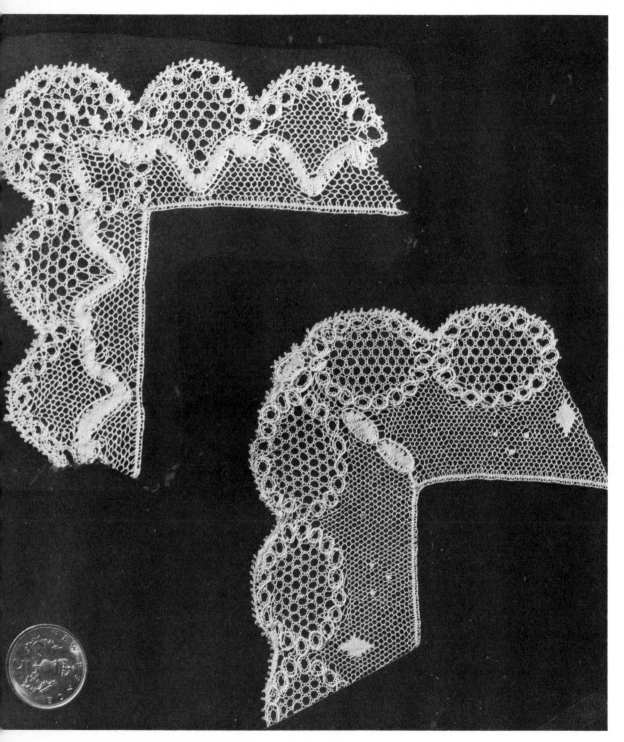

105 Corners of Bucks Point from traditional patterns including Honeycomb and Mayflower fillings. Worked by Mrs Betty Harrison, who teaches lacemaking to 30 students at one of the Sheffield Adult Education Centres.

106 Oval mat worked in ecru linen thread, using
16 bobbins, by Mrs Doreen Anderson, from a traditional Italian design, during her second year's work.

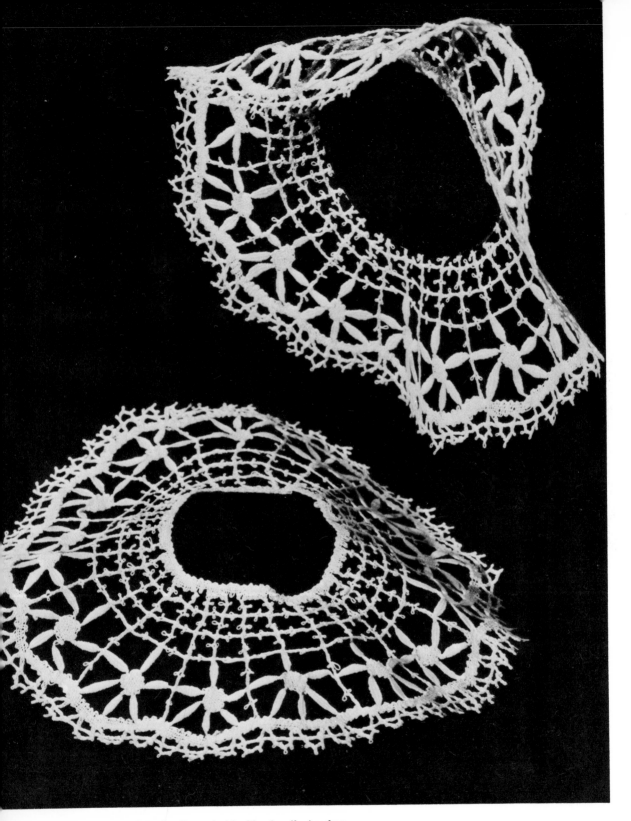

107 Pair of cuffs worked by Mrs Jennifer Lee from
an English pattern during her second year as a lace-
maker.

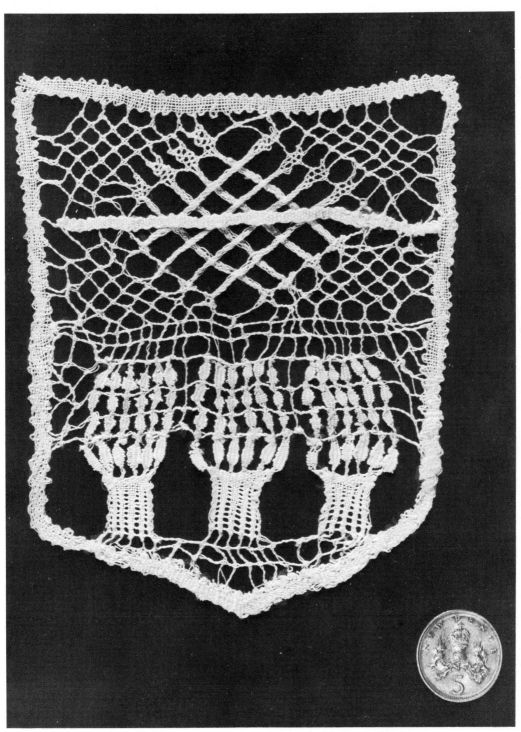

108 An adaptation of the shield from the arms of
the City of Sheffield, using traditional "cornseed"
(wheat grain) in the sheaves. Obviously other
heraldic coats, with their bold shapes, could be
re-created in terms of lace. Worked in 1972 by Mrs
Sybil Allan, first chairman of "Sheffield Lace-
Makers", founded 1973.

109 Square tablecloth with zodiac emblems, de-
signed and executed by Frau Professor Jaskolla,
Munich, Germany. By courtesy of the Museum of
Applied Art, New Collection, Munich. Photo: S. R.
Gramm, Munich.

110 *Tablecloth with flower motif, 1957. Concentric borders in white linen thread. Diameter 58 cm (about 23 in). By courtesy of the Museum of Arts and Crafts, Prague.*

111 Needlepoint lace, designed and executed by
Professor Emilie Palicková, Prague, 1930. Diameter
90 cm (about 35½ in). Photo: Milan Zemina.

122

112 *Detail of opposite picture.*

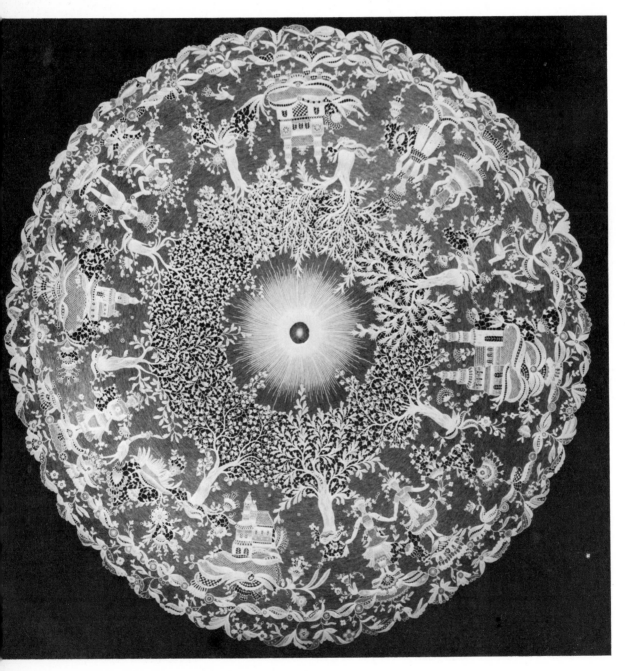

113   Needlepoint lace. Vladimir Holler (a legendary
hero). Designed and executed by Professor Emilie
Palicková, Prague. Diameter 150 cm (about 59 in).

114   Detail of opposite picture.

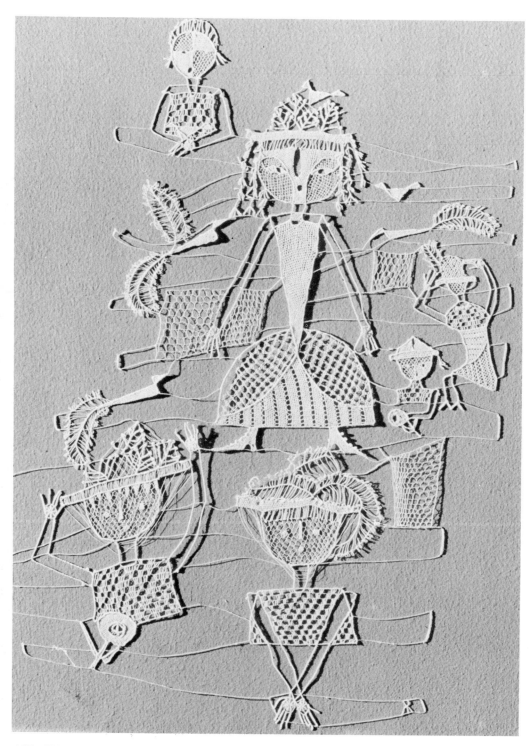

115 "Hat boutique", needlemade lace designed
and executed by Professor Hanne-Nüte Kämmerer,
1959. Art and Cultural History Museum, Oldenburg,
Germany. 32×24 cm (about $12\frac{1}{2} \times 9\frac{1}{2}$ in). Photo:
Wölbing van Dyck, Bielefeld.

116 "Garlands of pearls". Needlepoint by Professor
Hanne-Nüte Kämmerer, Münster-Detmold, 1962.
27×42 cm $(10\frac{3}{4} \times 16\frac{3}{4}$ in). Photo: Pan Walther,
Münster.

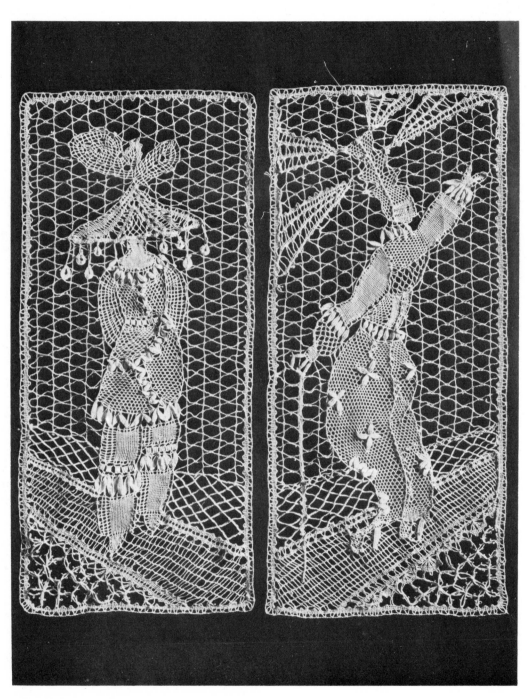

117   Bobbin lace motifs, 1920. Designed by Dagobert Peche and executed by the Vienna Workshops.
By courtesy of the Museum of Applied Art, Vienna.

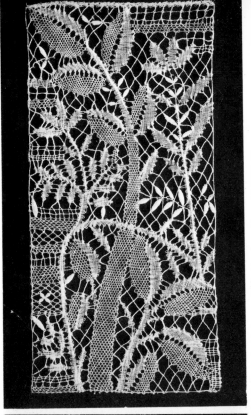

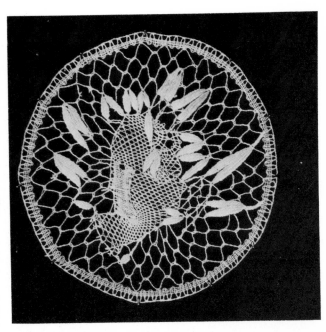

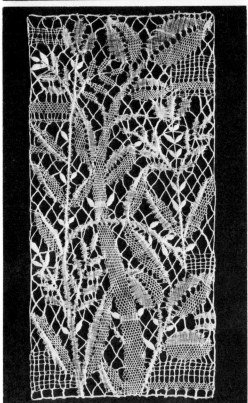

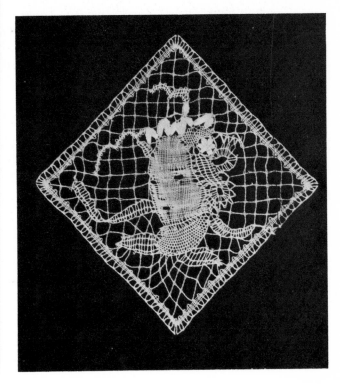

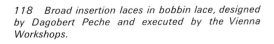

118 Broad insertion laces in bobbin lace, designed by Dagobert Peche and executed by the Vienna Workshops.

119 Two bobbin lace motifs designed by Dagobert Peche and executed by the Vienna Workshops, 1920.

120 "The Garden of Eden". Bobbin lace by Grete
Thums, Brno, Czechoslovakia. 27·5 × 32·5 cm (about
11 × 13 in). By courtesy of the Museum of Applied
Art, Vienna. See also p. 14.

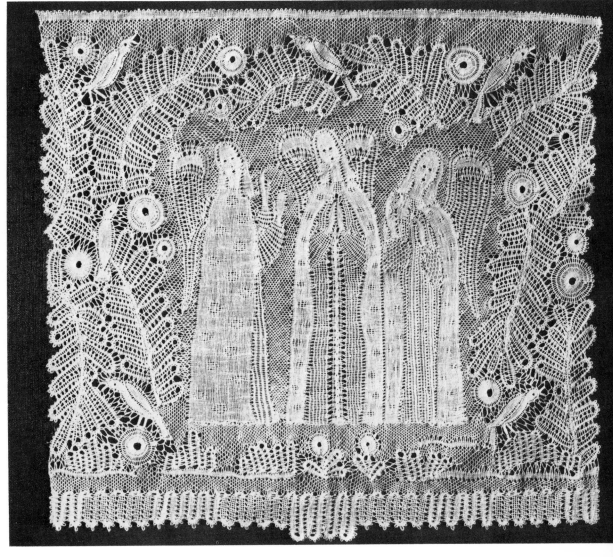

121 *"Singing Angels". Bobbin lace, designed and executed by Grete Thums, Brno, Czechoslovakia. 30 × 28·5 cm (about $11\frac{3}{4} × 11\frac{1}{4}$ in). By courtesy of the Museum of Applied Art, Vienna. Photo: Anton Fest.*

131

122 "The Annunciation". Bobbin lace designed
and executed by Grete Thums, Brno, Czechoslovakia.
By courtesy of the Museum of Applied Art, Vienna.

123 "Madonna". Bobbin lace designed and executed by Grete Thums, Brno, Czechoslovakia. By courtesy of the Museum of Applied Art, Vienna.

124 *"Palm Sunday". Bobbin lace designed and executed by Greta Sandberg, Sweden.*

125 *"Masked ball". Bobbin lace for a tea-table cloth by Suse Bernuth, Wuppertal, Germany, 1945. Photo: Abel-Menne.*

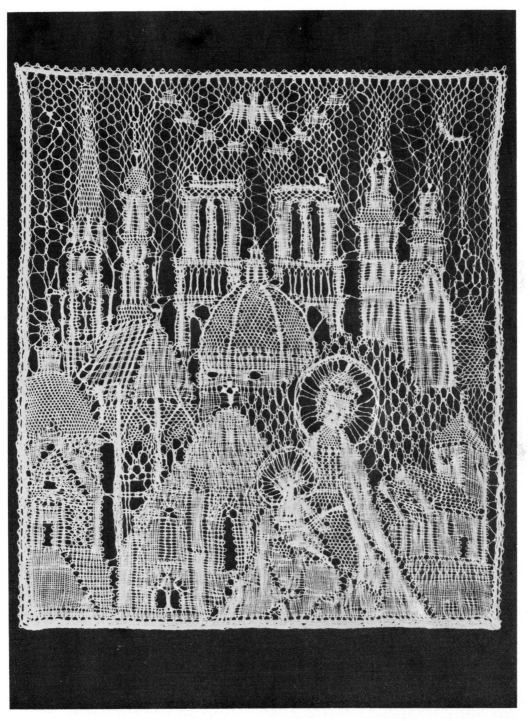

126 "The Virgin Mary in the grove". Bobbin lace
by Greta Sandberg, Sweden, 13·2 × 14·8 cm (about
5 × 5½ in).

127 Bobbin laces for church use. Designed by Suse Bernuth, Wuppertal, Germany, 1945. Executed by the State School of Bobbin Lace, Tiefenbach, Germany. Photo: Adolf Hierzegger, Berchtesgaden.

128 Bobbin lace traycloth in unbleached linen,
designed by Suse Bernuth, Wuppertal, Germany, and
executed by the State School of Bobbin Lace, Tiefen-   137
bach, Germany, 1945. Photo: Adolf Hierzegger,
Berchtesgaden. Proprietor: Institute for the Advancement of Crafts, Stuttgart.

129 ''Colibris'' (above) and part of a ''Four Seasons'' lace, designed by Suse Bernuth and executed by the Bobbin Lace School in Stadlern, Germany, Frau Kati Gruber 1945. About 15 cm (6 in) high. Cloth stitch and half stitch are among the techniques used.

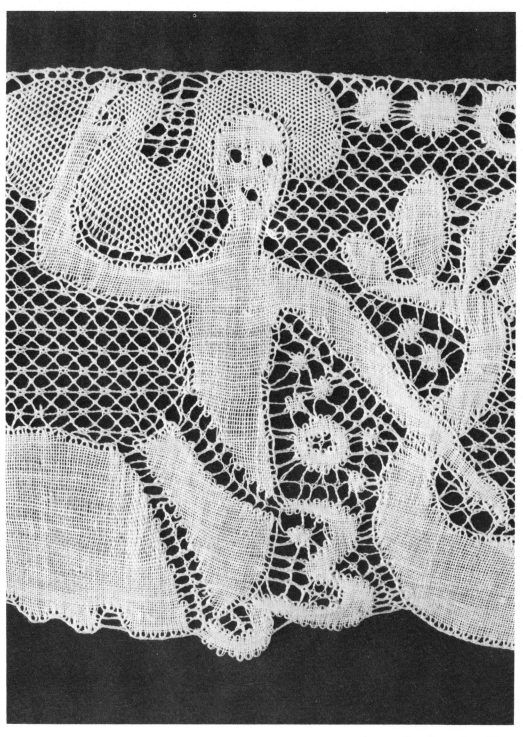

130 *Detail of the preceding illustration, "Four Seasons", 8 cm (about 3¼ in) high.*

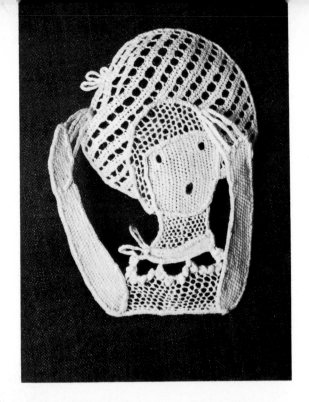

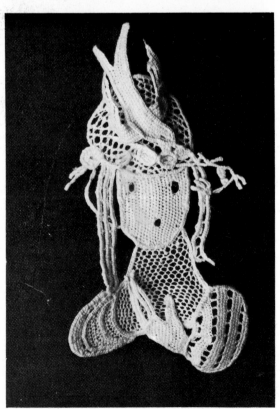

131 Two small picture motifs in needlepoint by Professor Hanne-Nüte Kämmerer, Detmold, Germany, 1948. Property: Ikle and Jakoby Collection, Crafts Museum, St Gallen, Switzerland, and private property. 8 cm (about 3¼ in) high. Photo: Pan Walther, Münster.

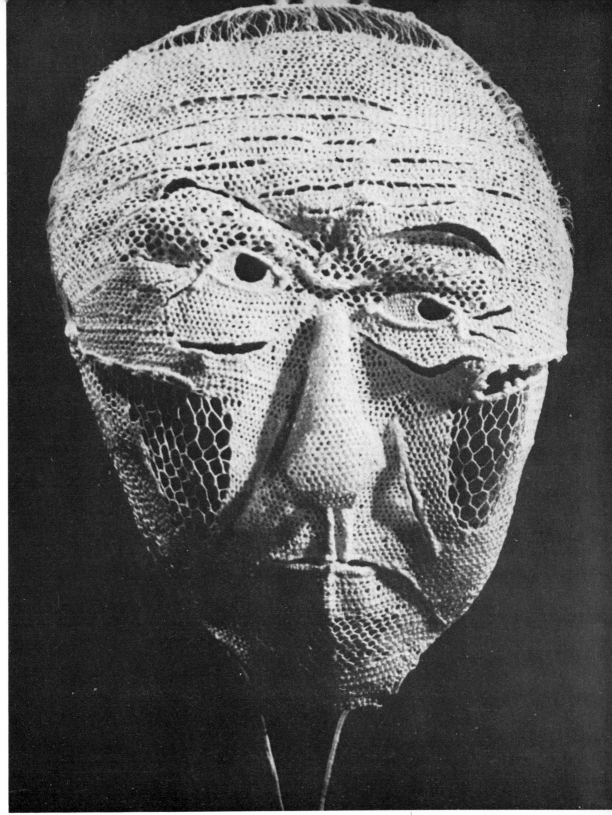

132 Needlepoint portrait of Herr Konrad Adenauer,
former Chancellor of Germany (15 September 1949–
15 October 1963), by Professor Hanne-Nüte   141
Kämmerer. 17 × 12 cm (about $6\frac{3}{4} \times 4\frac{3}{4}$ in). Property
of the artist. Photo: Pan Walther, Münster.

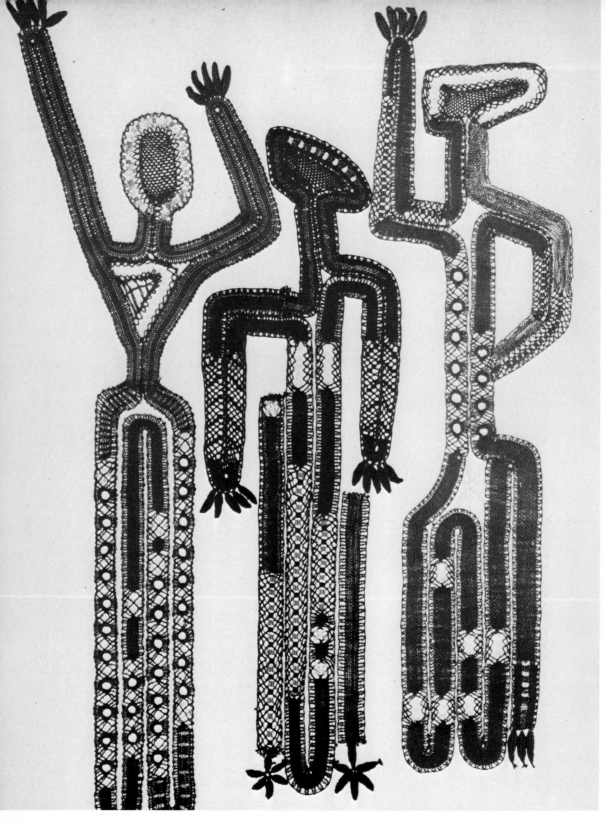

133 "The Three Graces". Braided lace in cotton perlé No. 5—black, violet, green, light blue, red and gold thread, designed and executed by Elena Holéczy, Bratislava, Czechoslovakia, 1965. 43×64 cm (about 17×25¼ in). Photo: Jozef Novy, Bratislava.

134 *"Aviary No. 1". Braided lace in handspun hemp and unbleached linen thread, designed and executed by Elena Holéczy, Bratislava, Czechoslovakia, 1965. 108 × 185 cm (about 42½ × 73 in). By courtesy of the Slovak National Gallery, Bratislava. Photo: Jozef Novy, Bratislava.*

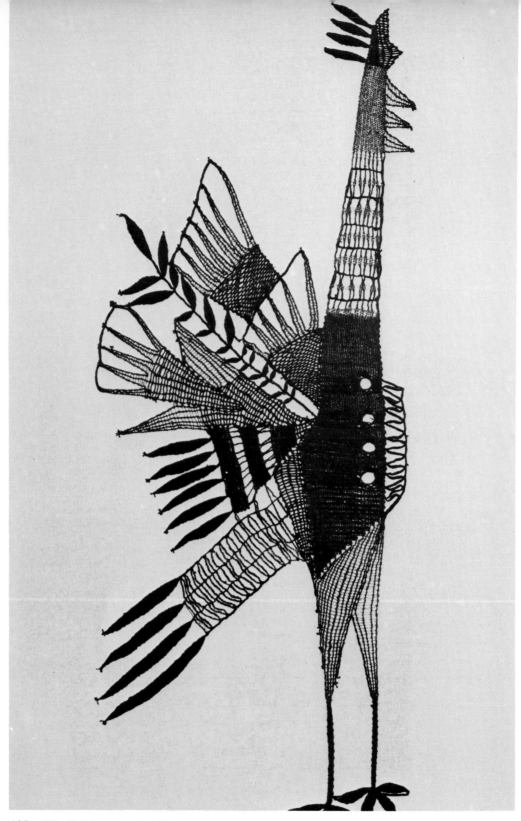

144   135   ''The Red Rooster''. Bobbin lace, gold threads added to red cotton and wool, designed and executed by Elena Holéczy, Bratislava, Czechoslovakia, 1965. 37×87 cm (about $14\frac{1}{2} \times 34\frac{1}{2}$ in). Photo: Jozef Novy, Bratislava.

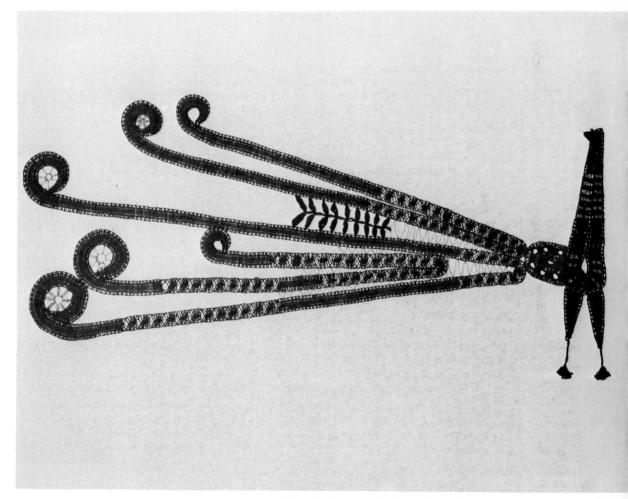

136 ''Red Peacock''. Braided lace in red cotton
perlé No. 5, black, and gold thread. Elena Holéczy,
Bratislava, Czechoslovakia.   145

137 "Peacocks" by Elena Holéczy, Bratislava, Czechoslovakia. Combination braid laces in white linen thread No. 250 with silver thread and multi-coloured bobbin lace, 1958. 20 × 28 cm (about 8 × 11 in). By courtesy of the Mahr Gallery, Brno, Czechoslovakia.

138 "Indian Summer"—a combination of needle
and bobbin laces in silver-grey, mid-grey and black
Berlin wool, designed and executed by Elena
Holéczy, Bratislava, Czechoslovakia, 1962. 99 × 139
cm (about $39 \times 54\frac{3}{4}$ in). By courtesy of the Slovak
National Gallery, Bratislava. Photo: Jozef Novy,
Bratislava.

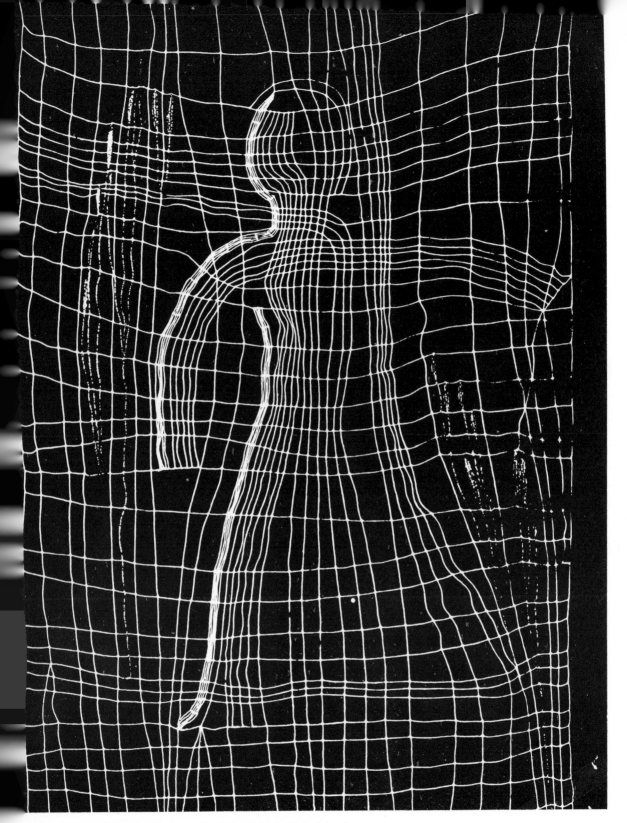

139   Detail of a needlepoint strip by Emilie Palicková
for the world exhibition Expo 58. From the book
Emilie Palicková by Ludmila Kybalová, published by
the Czech Publishing House for the Fine Arts, 1962.

140 Festival head-dress, designed by Marie Vankova-Kuchykova, Prague, and executed by the Vamberecka Kraijka Workshops, Vamberk, Czechoslovakia. Exhibited at Expo 67, Montreal. 70 cm (about 27½ in) wide. Bobbin lace with relief effects in silver and gold threads, linen and beads. By courtesy of the Museum of Lace, Vamberk.

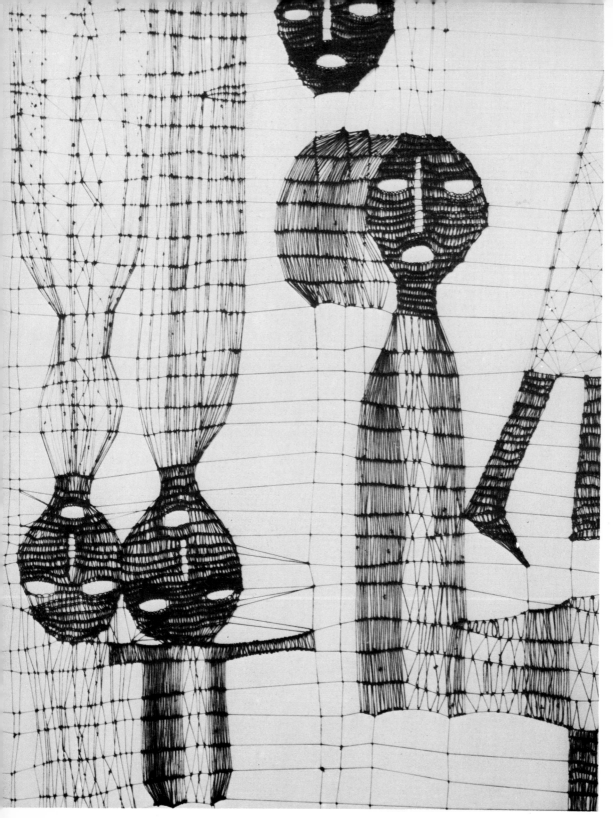

141 Detail of a lace wall hanging, ''Carnival'' by
Luba Krecji, Prague, 1959.

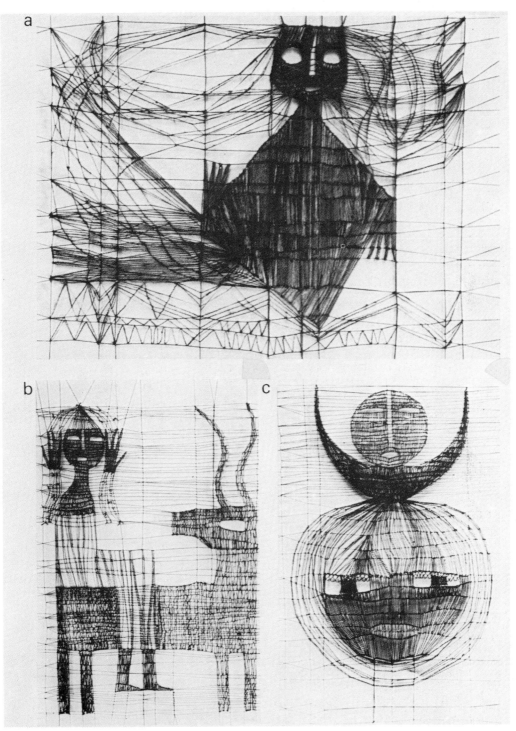

142 Three more works designed and executed by
Luba Krecji in hemp and linen thread:
    (a) "Forgotten". Blue-green.
    (b) "Snowfall", black and indigo. 40×30 cm
        (about $15\frac{3}{4} \times 11$ in).

(c) "Evening star looking for the moon", pinky-
    mauve. 40×30 cm (about $15\frac{3}{4} \times 11$ in).
Photos: K. Zastera, Prague.

143 Two further works designed and executed by
Luba Krecji in hemp and linen thread:
  *"The crimson bird". Red and pink. 220 × 220
  cm (about 87 in square).*
  Photos: K. Zastera, Prague.

144 *"Red umbrellas" by Luba Krecji. By courtesy
of the National Gallery, Prague. Photo: Majka
Pavlikova.*

145 *"The King's Knights", designed and executed by Hana Klima-Kralova, Ezra Ubizaron, Israel. 1960. 150 × 250 cm (about 59 × 98 in). Natural-coloured thread.*

154 146 (a) and (b). "Between Heaven and Earth",
multi-coloured red bobbin lace by Hana Klima-
Kralova, Prague. 1951. 90 × 120 cm (about 35½ ×
47¼ in). This piece, mounted between two pieces of
glass, has been photographed from both front and
back. By courtesy of the National Gallery, Prague.
Photos: (a) Jan Sirovy, (b) Maja Pavlikova.

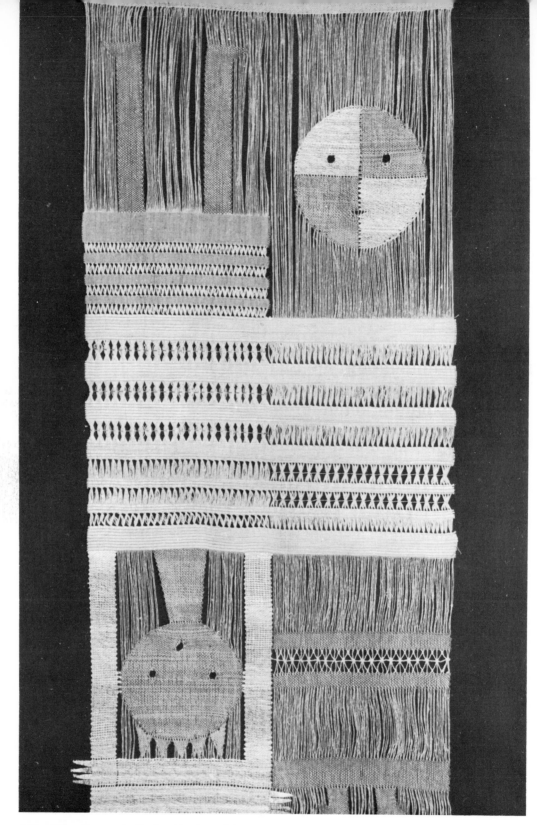

147 *"The Moonseeker". Combination of bobbin lace and weaving, designed and executed by Hana Klima-Kralova, Ezra Ubizaron, Israel. 1964. White and blue and natural thread. 50×110 cm (about $19\frac{3}{4}×43\frac{1}{4}$ in).*

148 *"The little King", red bobbin lace by Hana Klima-Kralova, Ezra Ubizaron, Israel. 1964. 25 × 60 cm (about 10 × 23¾ in).*

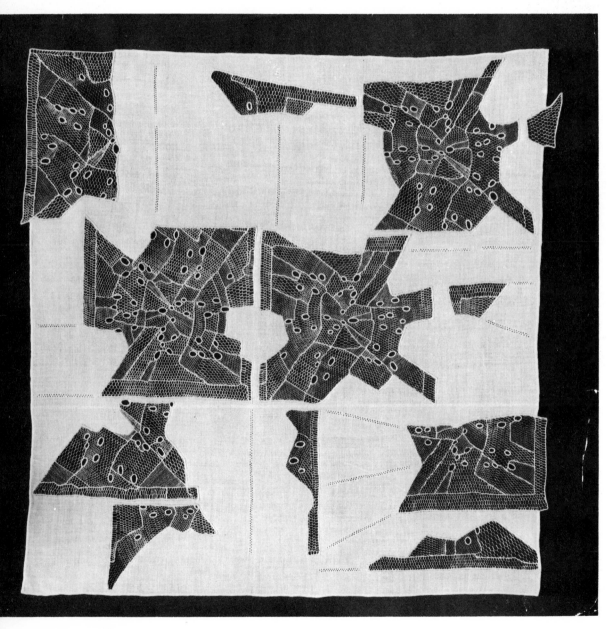

149 Batiste handkerchief with needlepoint, designed and executed by Bohumila Gruskorska. 28 ×
28 cm (about 11 in square). By courtesy of the
Skolsky Institute for Arts and Crafts, Prague. Photo:
Milan Zemina, Prague.

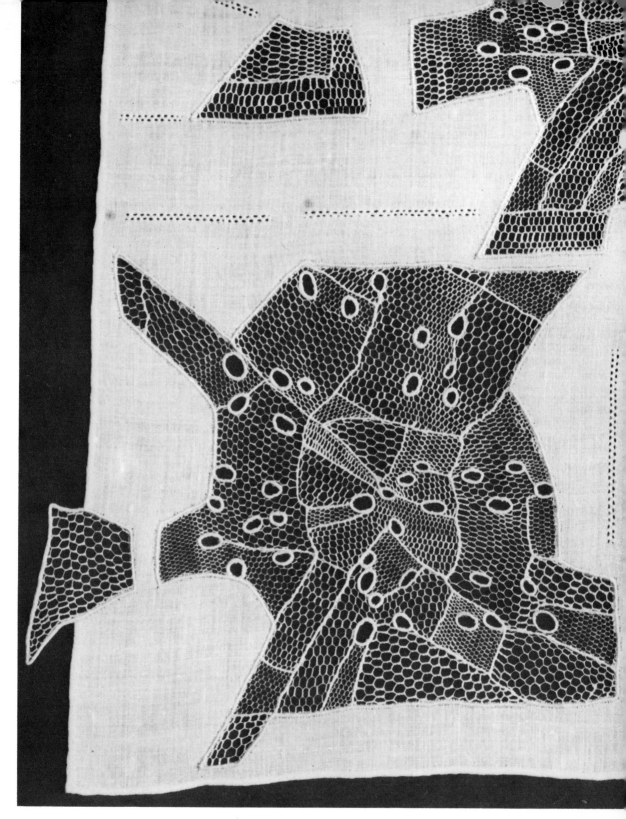

150 *A detail from the preceding work.*

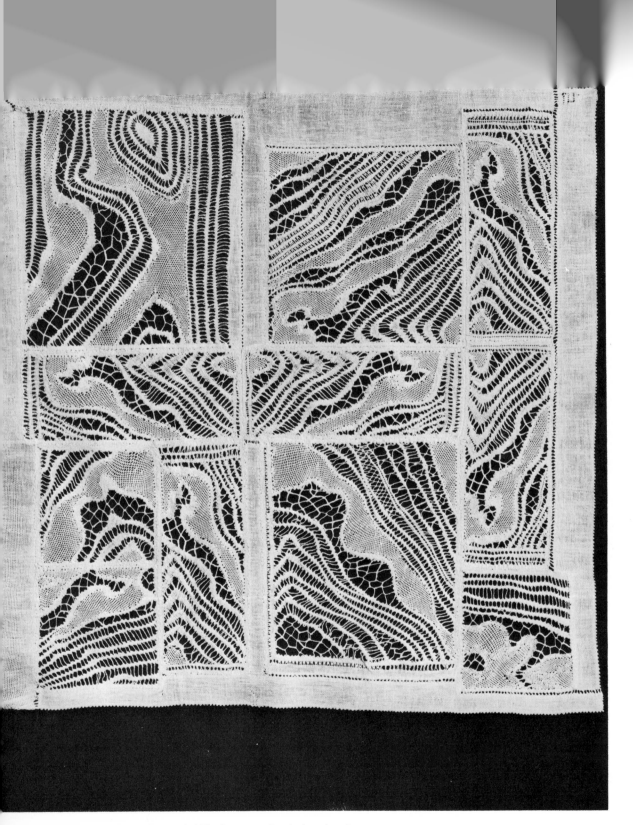

151 "Life", a bobbin lace sampler designed and
executed by Leni Matthaei, Reutlingen, Germany.
60 × 60 cm (about 23½ in square). 1964. Has been
bought by the municipality of Reutlingen. Photo:
Traute Uhland-Klaus.

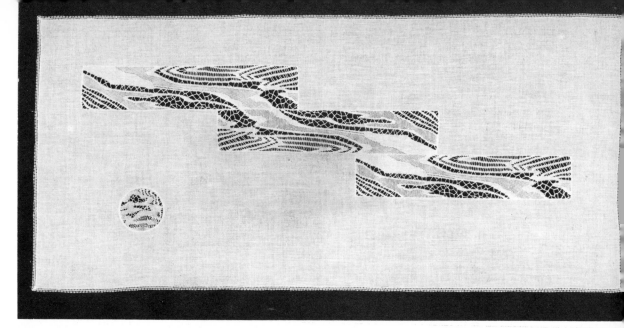

152 "Stream", designed and executed by Leni Matthaei, Reutlingen, Germany. Bobbin lace. 95 × 35 cm (37 × 14 in). Winner of Bavarian State Prize and gold medal in International Fair, 1967.

The following two photographs show (a) a detail and (b) a variant which won a prize in its class at the handicraft exhibition held in Constance, West Germany, in 1972. Photos: Traute Uhland-Klaus Näher.

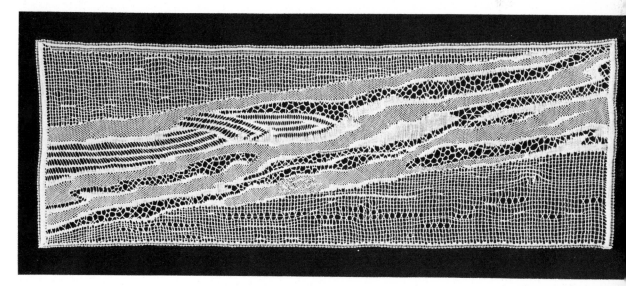

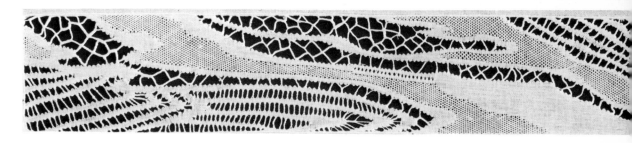

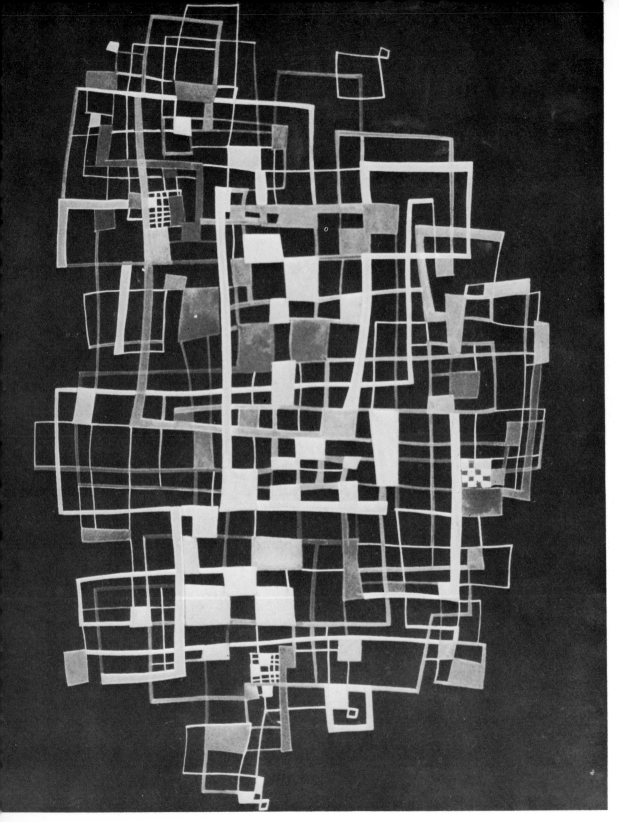

153   Design for a needlepoint in ''punto Burano''
by Bice Lazzari Rosa, Rome, 1954.

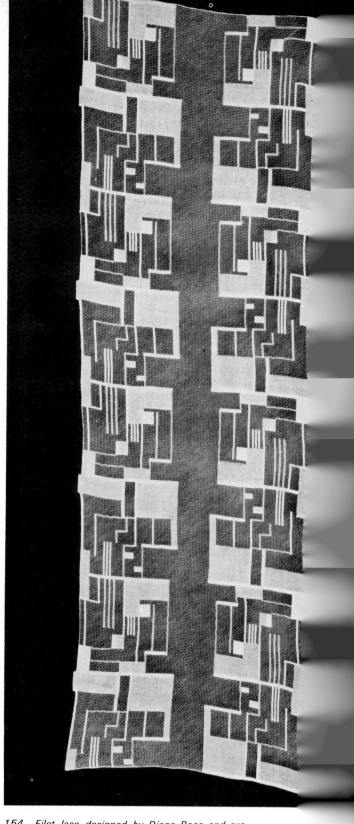

154 *Filet lace designed by Diego Rosa and exe-cuted by Sara Vasile, Isnello, Palermo, Sicily.*

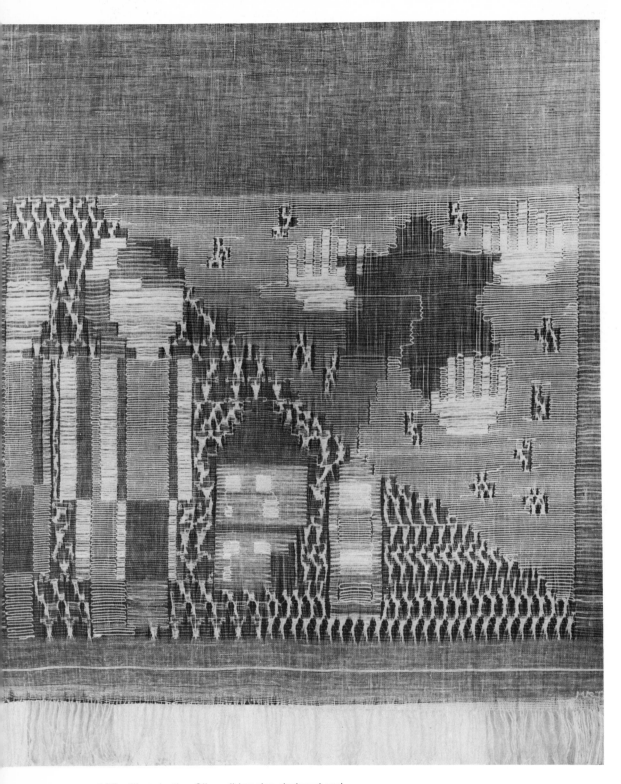

155 "Imagination 2", wall-hanging designed and
executed by Hedwig Klöckner-Triebe, Münster, Germany, combining lace technique with weaving.
Linen, 73 × 79 cm (about 28¾ × 31 in). 1962.

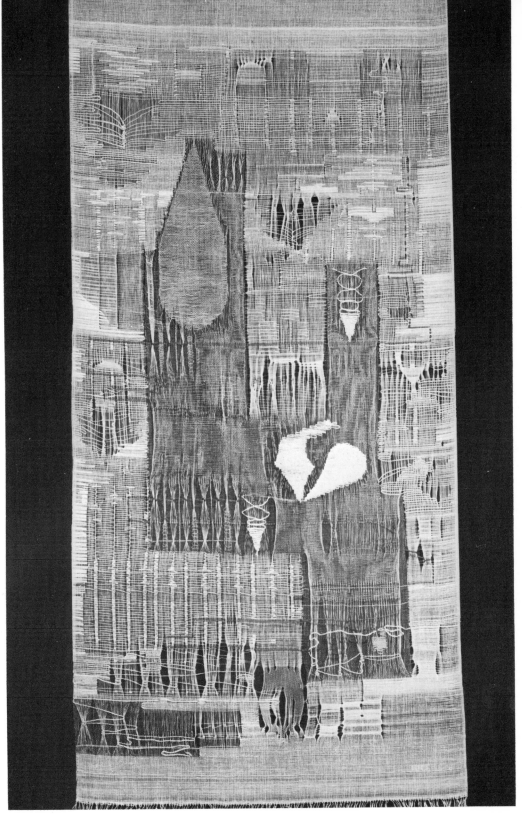

156 *"The drop that falls upon the earth", wall hanging designed and executed by Hedwig Klöckner-Triebe, Münster, Germany, in lace-type weave. Linen, 97 × 200 cm (about 38¼ × 79 in). 1963. By courtesy of the Folk Art Council, Stuttgart, Germany. Photo: Bathe.*

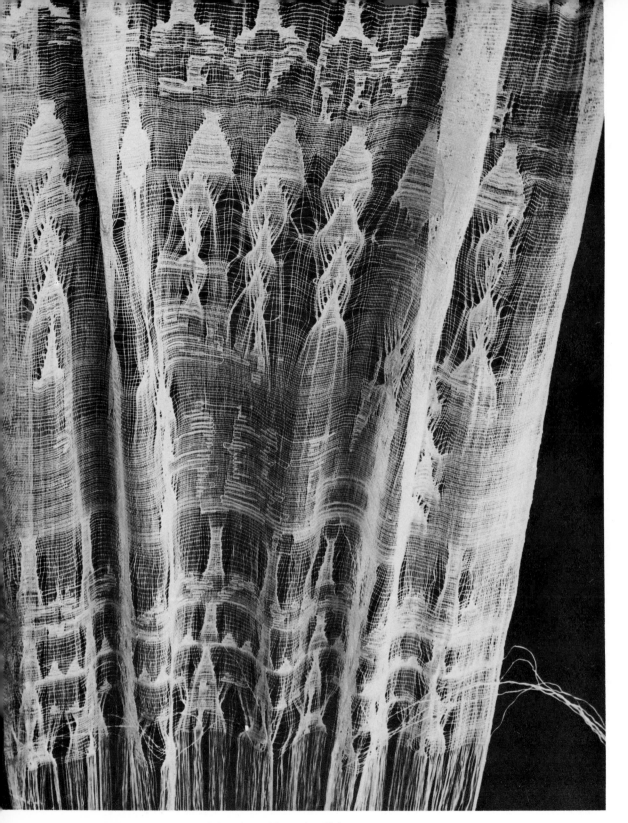

157 *Detail of a wall hanging with work still in progress. 1960. Design and execution by Hedwig Klöckner-Triebe, Münster, Germany. Photo: Ulla Heinz, Hagen.*

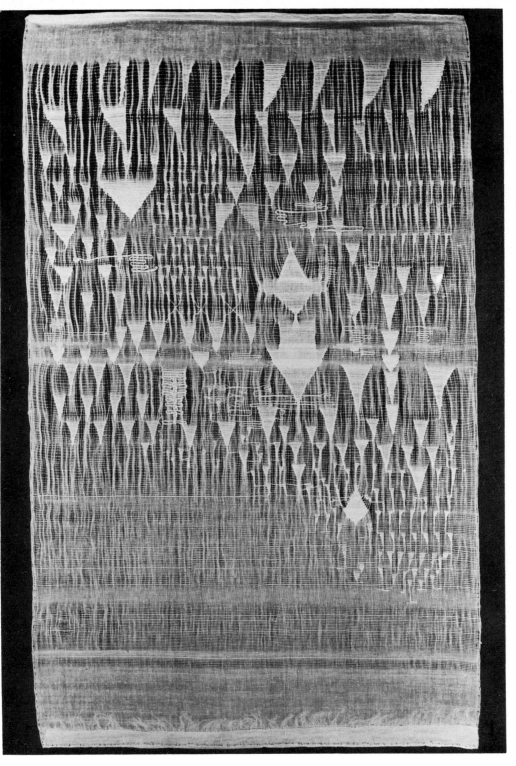

158 Wall hanging designed and executed by
Hedwig Klöckner-Triebe, Münster, Germany, in a
lace-type weave. Linen, 70×110 cm (about 27½×
43¼ in). Photo: Pan Walther, Münster. 1967.

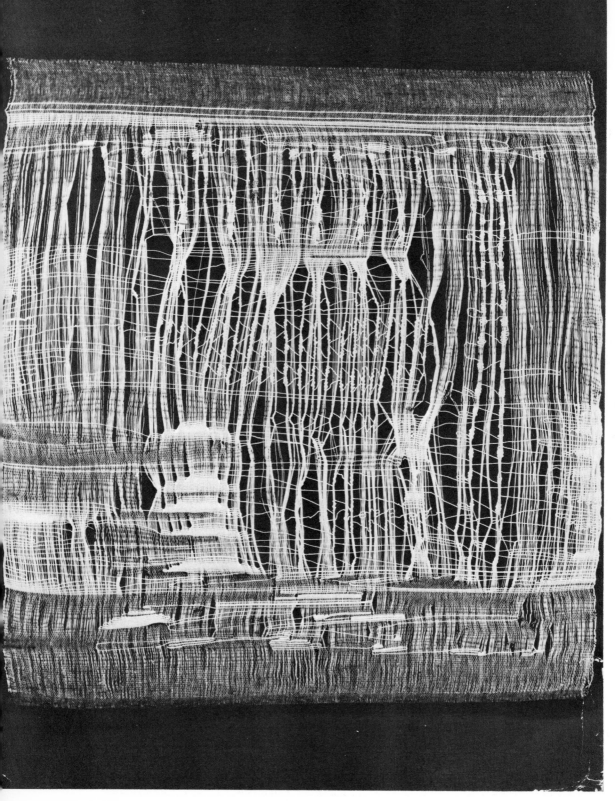

159 "Abstract", wall hanging designed and executed by Hedwig Klöckner-Triebe, Münster, Germany. 1960. Property of the German Foreign Office. 76×79 cm (about $30 \times 31\frac{1}{4}$ in). Photo: Pan Walther, Münster.

160 "Nightblossom", wall hanging designed and executed by Hedwig Klöckner-Triebe, Münster, Germany, in a lace-type weave. 1966. Linen and silk, 35 × 45 cm (about 14 × 18 in). Property of the German Foreign Office. Photo: Pan Walther, Münster.

Textile Kostbarkeiten

Gems of Textile Handicraft

«De Fil en Aiguille»
Broderies, Dentelles, Tissages

161 Textile graphic for a catalogue cover. The original was in cotton, knitted, knotted and embroidered by Barbara Retzlaff-Poika, Stuttgart, Germany.

162 *"Structural fragment", lace-type weaving designed and executed by Hedwig Klöckner-Triebe,* *Münster, Germany. Silk, in greyish-purple and brown, 25·5 × 25·5 cm (about 10 in square) 1968.*

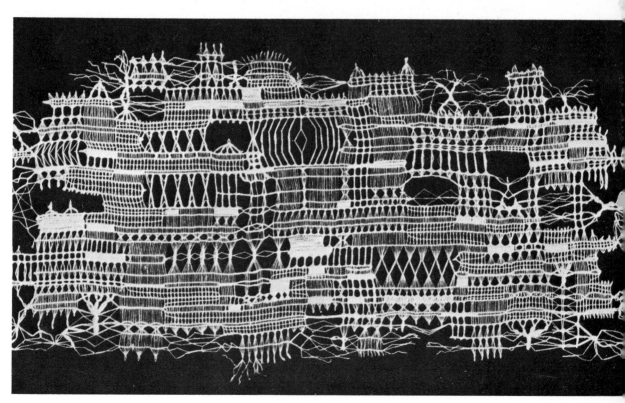

163 *"Memories", appliqué with openwork by Maria Benatzky-Tillman, Cologne. White on black linen, 80 × 37 cm (about 31½ × 14½ in).*

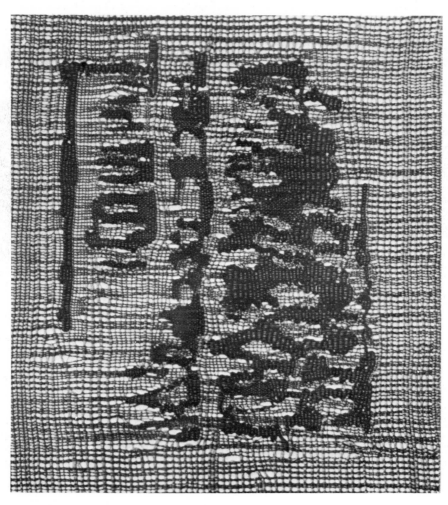

164 ''Light in darkness'', lace-type weave designed and executed by Hedwig Klöckner-Triebe, Münster, Germany. Deep reds and greens on a greyish-purple background. Mercerised cotton and linen, 26·5 × 26·5 cm (about 10½ in square). 1968.

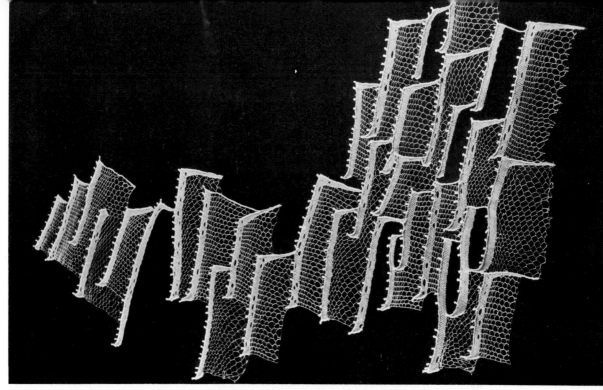

165 "Hieroglyphs", needlepoint by Professor Hanne-Nüte Kämmerer, Detmold, Germany. Linen, 35 × 21 cm (about $13\frac{1}{2} \times 8\frac{1}{4}$ in). Property of the German Foreign Office. 1961.

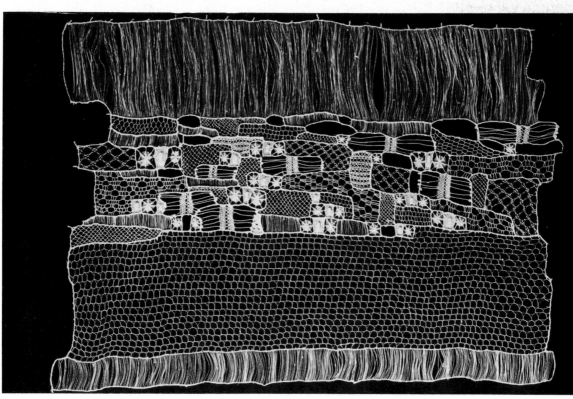

166 "Little Garden", needlepoint designed and executed by Professor Hanne-Nüte Kämmerer, Detmold, Germany. 20 × 30 cm (about $8\frac{3}{4} \times 11\frac{3}{4}$ in). Property of the Landesgewerbeamt (institute of Crafts), Stuttgart. 1958. Photo: Pan Walther, Münster, Germany.

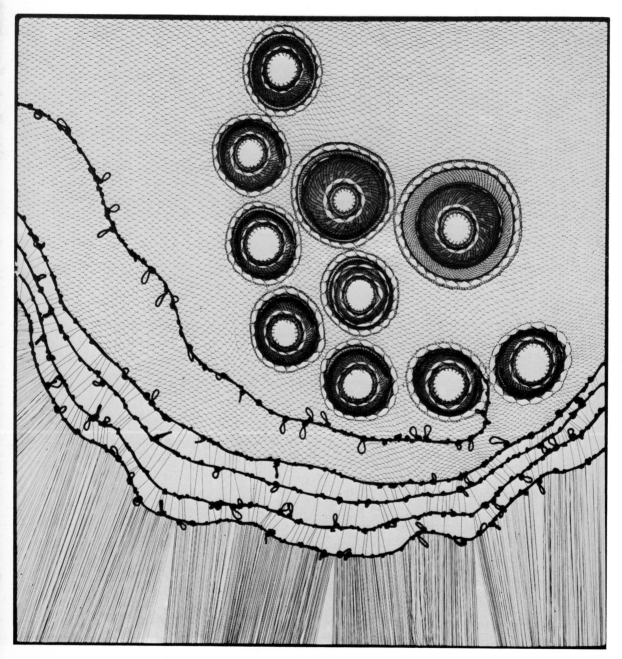

167 Room divider in black lace, designed and executed by Professor Hanne-Nüte Kämmerer, Detmold, Germany. Some plastics are incorporated in tightly stretched frames. 1964. 140 × 140 cm (about 55 in square). Photo: H. Vössing, Münster. Property of the artist.

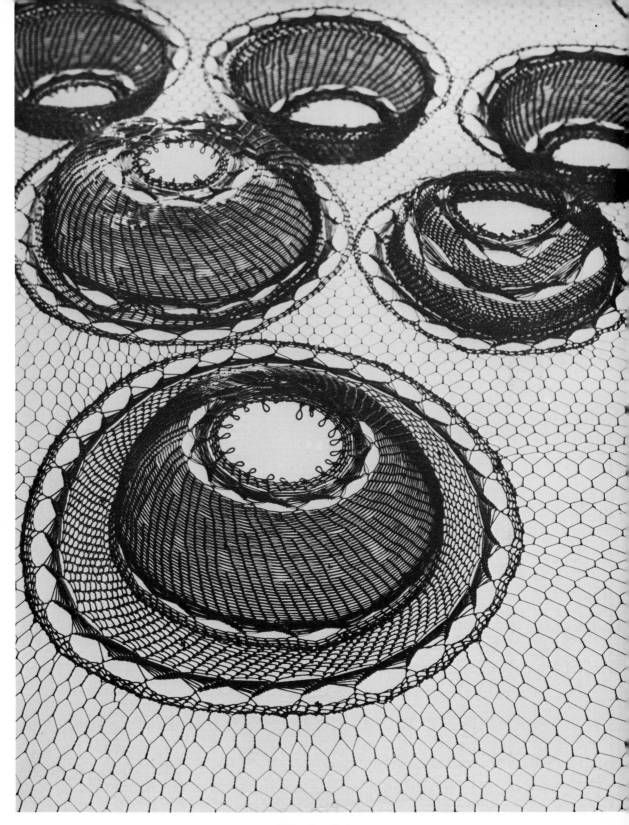

168   *Detail of the preceding piece.*

169 *"Mirrors", designed and executed by Professor*
Hanne-Nüte Kämmerer, Detmold, Germany, 1969.
Needlepoint. Three-dimensional forms stretched in
a frame. Tiny pieces of mirror glass are mounted in
the "peaks" of the shapes. 60×60 cm (about $23\frac{1}{2}$ in
square). Property of the artist. Photo: Susanne
Walther, Münster.

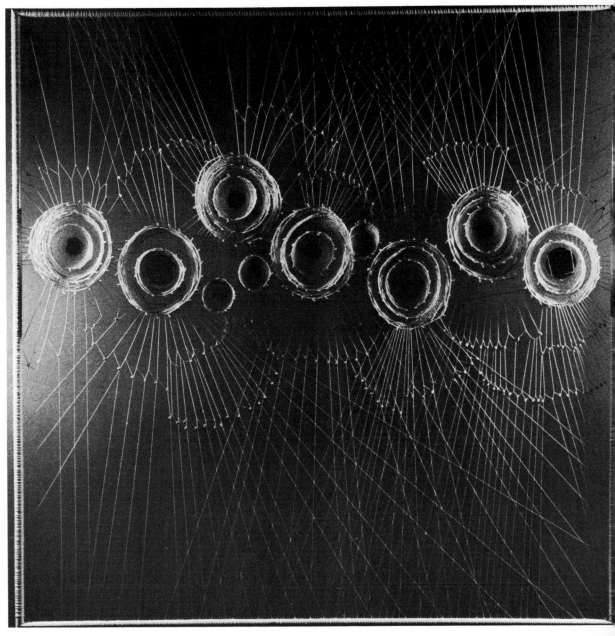

170 "Waterlilies", needlepoint stretched on a frame. Designed and executed by Professor Hanne-Nüte Kämmerer, Detmold, Germany. 1969. 60 × 60 cm (about 23½ in square). Property of the artist. Photo: Susanne Walther, Münster.

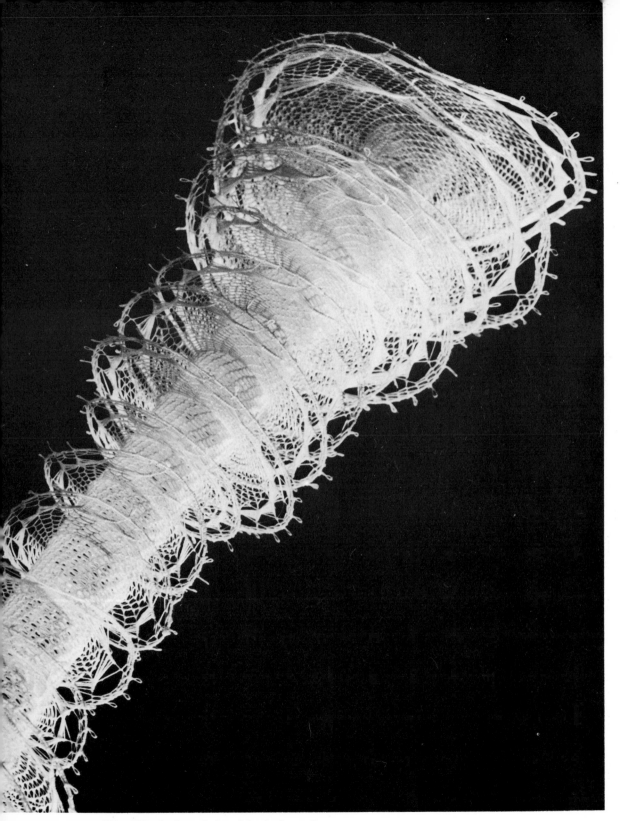

171 "Plastic Form in Lace" by Professor Hanne-
Nüte Kämmerer, Detmold, Germany. Photo: Susanne
Walther, Münster.

172 "Signal Tower". Needlepoint around cylinder
of glass 30 cm (about 11¾ in) high, by Professor
Hanne-Nüte Kämmerer, Detmold, Germany. 1968.   179
Photo: Susanne Walther, Münster.

173 Three-dimensional free-hanging lace "Fountain", designed by Marie Vankova-Kuchynkova, Prague, and executed by the Vamberecka Krajka Workshops in Vamberk, Czechoslovakia. Linen, 1 metre (just over a yard) in diameter and 6 metres high. This black and white bobbin lace was worked in two straight pieces and then suspended to create a three-dimensional form. Exhibited in Expo 67, Montreal. By courtesy of the Museum of Lace, Vamberk.

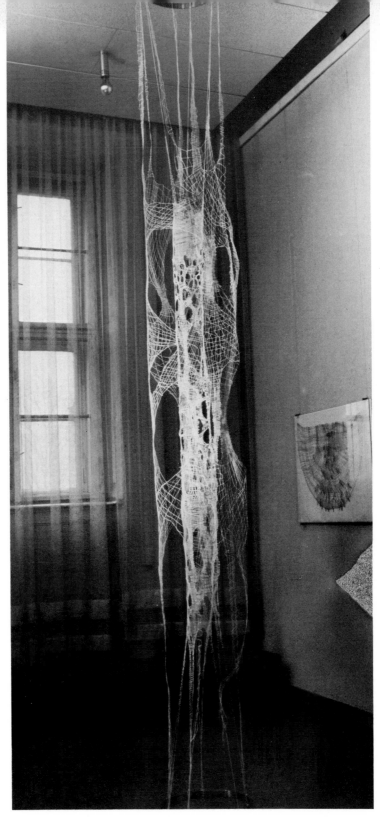

174 "Space Lace" designed by Marie Vankova-Kuchynkova, Prague, and executed by Marie Vankova and the Vamberecka Krajka Workshops in Vamberk. Linen, white and silver, diameter 40 cm, height 4·5 metres (about 15¾ in and a little under 5 yards). Made 1969, exhibited in the 5th Biennale, Lausanne, 1971. Now owned by the Museum of Arts and Crafts, Prague.

175 Three-dimensional free-hanging lace designed and executed by Marie Vankova-Kuchynkova, Prague, 1968. Diameter 28 cm (about 11 in). Worked as bobbin lace, in two parts over a spherical form. Black and white linen in threads of two different thicknesses.

176 *Three-dimensional lace designed and executed by Marie Vankova-Kuchynkova, Prague, 1968. White and silver linen. The lace was worked with bobbins as a straight piece and one point was then pulled through a space left for the purpose. By courtesy of the Museum of Lace, Vamberk.*

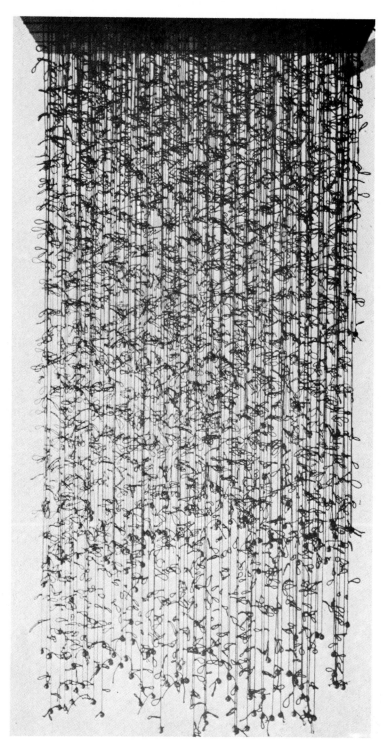

177 ''Knotted Strings'', three-dimensional wall
hanging in black cotton. Designed and executed by
Sofie Dawo, Saarbrücken, Germany, 1964. 50 × 100
× 30 cm (about $19\frac{3}{4} \times 39\frac{1}{2} \times 11\frac{3}{4}$ in).

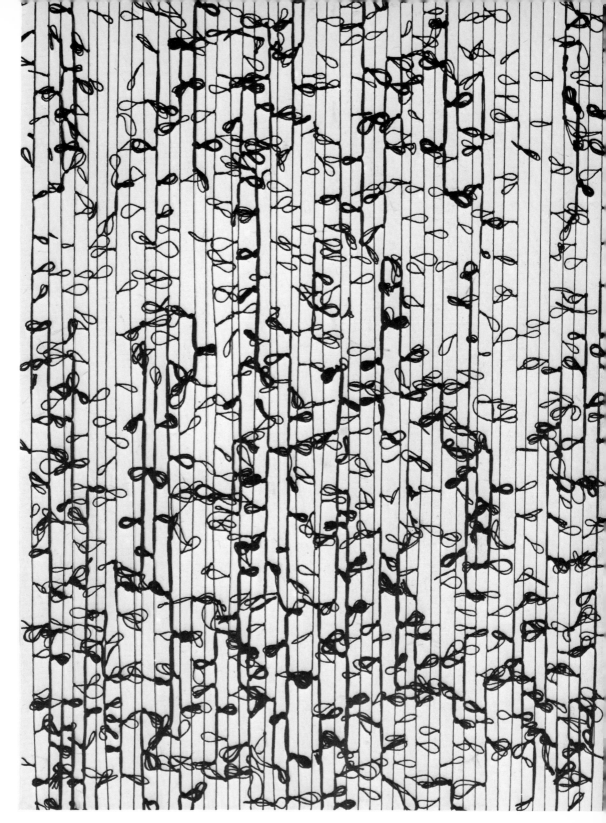

178 ''Textile graphic'' detail. Knotted on white
carton. Designed and executed by Sofie Dawo,
Saarbrücken, Germany, 1965. 50×70 cm (about
$19\frac{3}{4} \times 27\frac{1}{2}$ in).

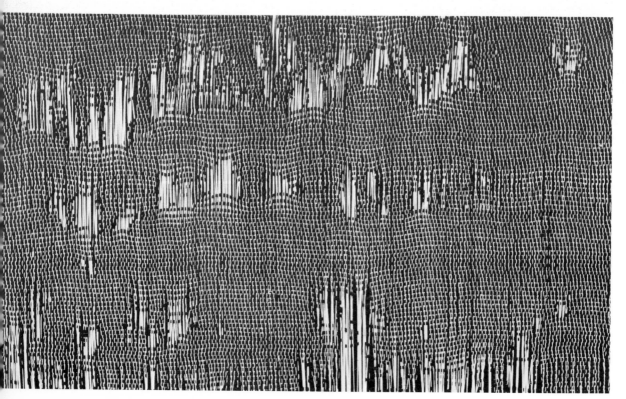

179 Woven wall hanging designed and executed
by Sofie Dawo, Saarbrücken, Germany, 1969/70.
White lastex warp, black wool weft. 116 × 105 cm
(about $45\frac{3}{4} \times 41\frac{1}{4}$ in).

180 Woven wall hanging designed and executed
by Sofie Dawo, Saarbrücken, Germany, 1963. Blue
and white wool, 130 × 130 cm (about 51 in square).   187
Property of the Ministry of Culture, Saarbrücken.

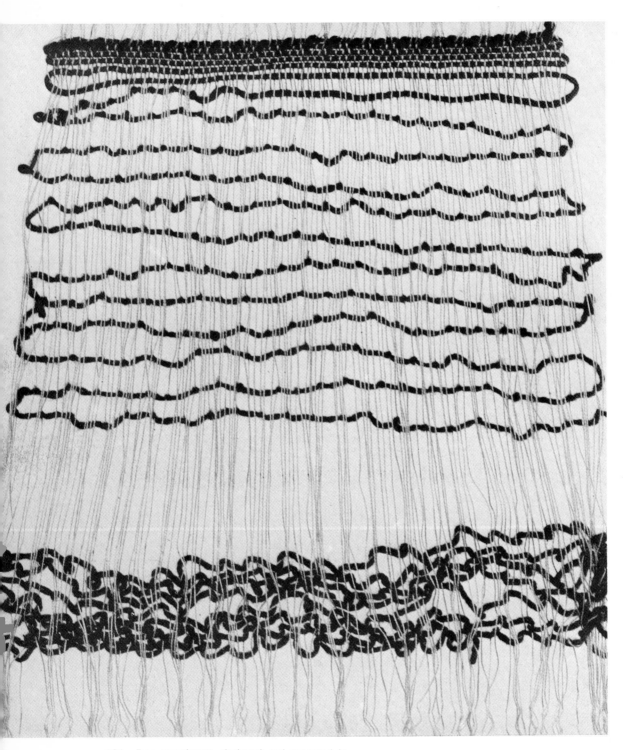

181 Free experiment, designed and executed by
Sofie Dawo, Saarbrücken, Germany, 1963. White
cotton warp and black wool weft. 60 × 40 cm (about
$23\frac{3}{4} \times 15\frac{3}{4}$ in) knotted.

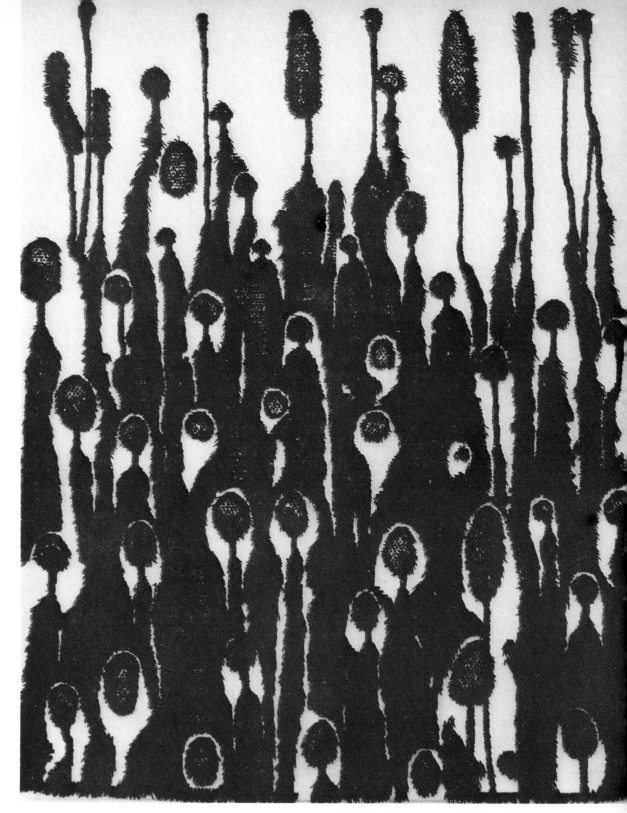

182 Wall hanging designed by Sofie Dawo, Saarbrücken, Germany, and executed by the Sindelfingen
School of Weaving. The three-dimensional design,
of various thicknesses, is carried out in mixed techniques on a white tapestry ground. 1964. 225 × 285
cm (about $88\frac{3}{4} \times 112\frac{1}{2}$ in). Property of the District
Savings Bank, Blieskastel, Germany.

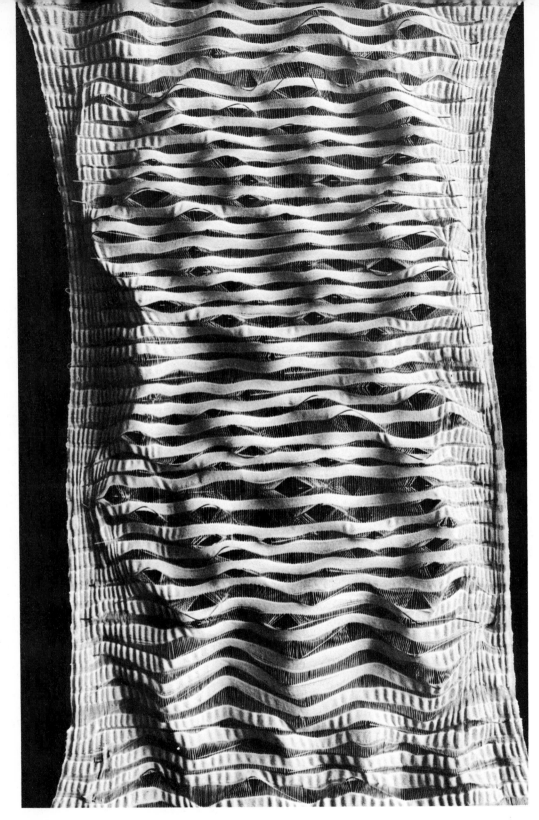

183 Wall hanging designed and executed by Sofie Dawo, Saarbrücken, Germany, 1970. In a mixture of techniques, it has a white lastex ribbon warp and a weft of white wool and silvered steel. 140 × 90 cm (about 55 × 35½ in).

184 *Detail of the preceding piece.*

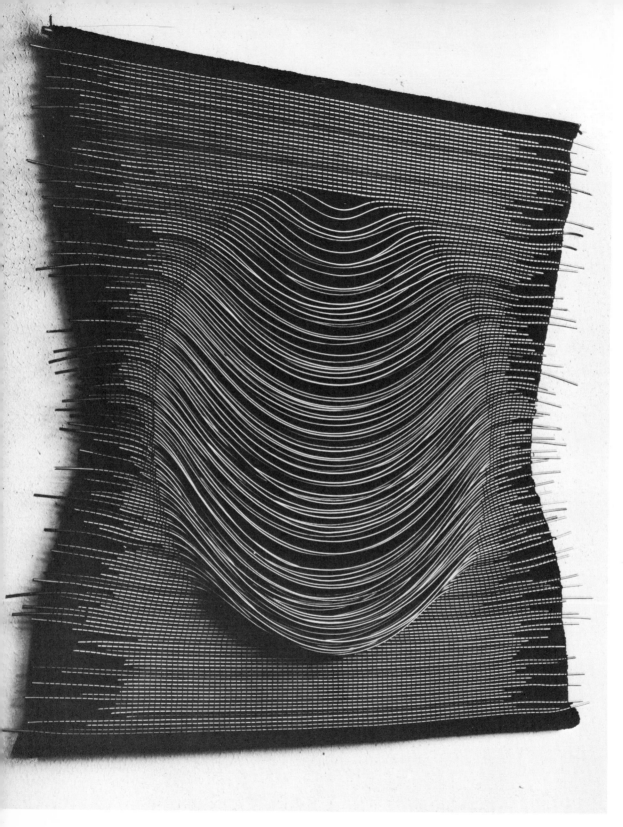

185 "Metal Spirals" hanging designed and executed by Sofie Dawo, Saarbrücken, Germany, 1966.
Flexible rods of silver, blue, violet and brown are
interwoven with black wool and black cotton. 124 ×
120 cm (about $48\frac{1}{4} \times 47\frac{1}{4}$ in).

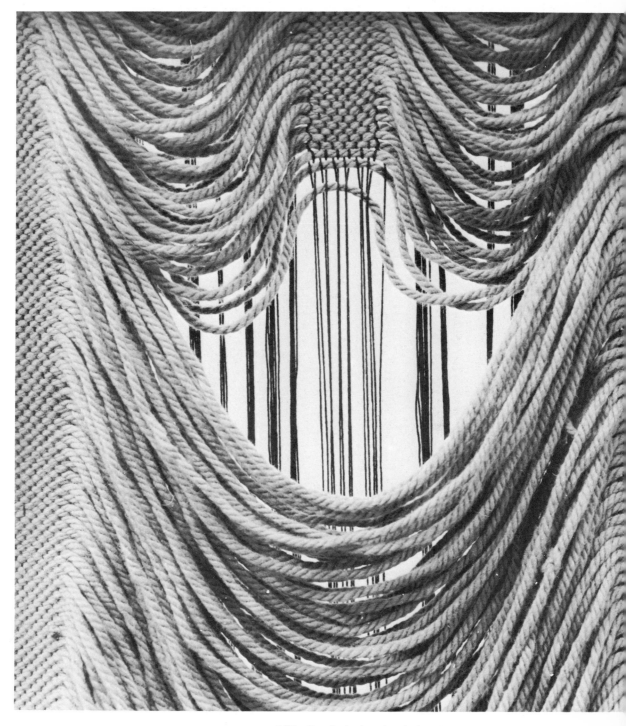

186   Detail of a hanging designed and executed by
Sofie Dawo, Saarbrücken, Germany, 1967. Black
cotton warp and blue Smyrna weft. 157 × 66 cm
(about 62 × 26 in). Photo: W. Klein.

187 ''Free Experiment'', designed and executed by
Sofie Dawo, Saarbrücken, Germany, 1964. White
cotton warp with a black wool weft. 30 × 40 cm
(about 12 × 16 in). Photo: H. Boockmann.

188 Detail of a white knotted rug, designed and
executed by Sofie Dawo, Saarbrücken, Germany,
1967. The rug is 80 × 295 cm (about 31½ × 116 in).

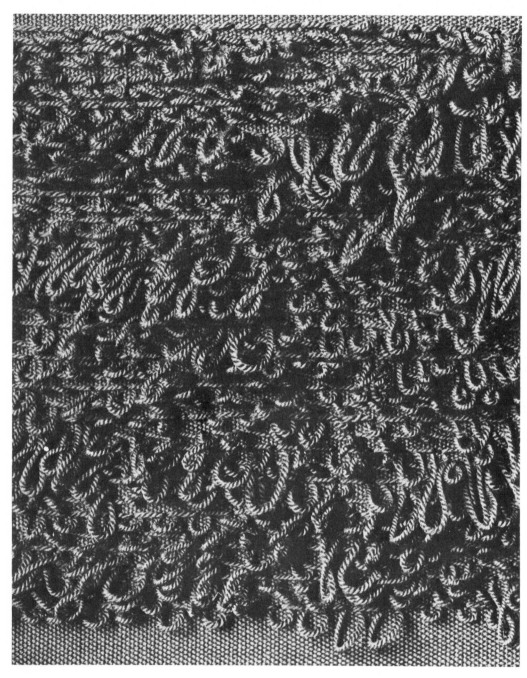

189 Hanging in a knotted technique, designed and
executed by Sofie Dawo, Saarbrücken, Germany,
1967. Black wool. 80 × 80 cm (about 31 in square).

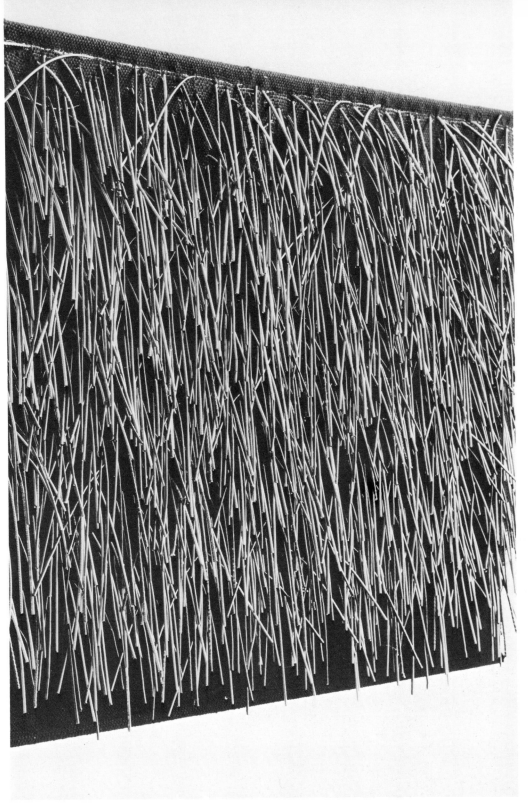

190 "Metal coils", wall hanging designed and executed by Sofie Dawo, Saarbrücken, Germany, 1971. The warp is black cotton and the weft black Smyrna wool with brown, silver and blue metal coils. 114 × 120 cm (about 45 × 47¼ in).

191 *"Captive Comet", macramé lace designed and
executed by Aurelia Munoz, Barcelona, 1971. White
linen, 40 × 40 × 40 cm (a cube of about $15\frac{3}{4}$ in).
Photo: Ramón Calvet.*

192 *Detail of preceding piece. Photo: José Ven-
tosa.*

193 "Macra Bird", designed and executed by
Aurelia Munoz, Barcelona, 1970. Macramé lace in
black wool and white linen, 200 × 130 cm (about
79 × 51 in). Photo: Ramón Calvet.

194 *"Macra metamorphosis", designed and exe-cuted by Aurelia Munoz, Barcelona, 1972. White cotton string, 218 × 200 cm (about 86 × 79 in). In the Miguel Adria Collection, Barcelona. Photo: Ramón Calvet.*

195 "Webs", wall hanging designed and executed
by Maryke Stultiens, Bunde, Holland. Sisal rope and
wool, black and gold, 300 × 500 cm (about 118 ×
197 in).